THE NAVY

THE NAVY

"Semper Fortis"

ANDREW WIEST

amber
BOOKS

Published by Amber Books Ltd
United House
North Road
London N7 9DP
United Kingdom
www.amberbooks.co.uk
Instagram: amberbooksltd
Facebook: amberbooks
Twitter: @amberbooks
Pinterest: amberbooksltd

ISBN: 978-1-83886-059-2

Project Editor: Michael Spilling
Designer: Mark Batley
Picture Research: Terry Forshaw

Printed in China

Contents

The Modern Navy

Based on the precepts of the storied naval theorist, Alfred Thayer Mahan, the modern U.S. Navy is designed to command the common spaces between nations so that the high seas are free and open to all. With traditions that date back to the seafarers of the mighty British fleet and through colonial times, the U.S. Navy traces its operational history to the Continental Navy that stood toe-to-toe with its British forbearers. As the nation came of age, so did the Navy—a truly daunting task, with two vast oceans on its doorstep and with a worldwide mandate. By World War II, the U.S. Navy supplanted that of Britain as the largest in the world.

Today's U.S. Navy is historically dominant, larger than the next 13 fleets in the world combined. With nearly 300 combat vessels and 4,000 aircraft, the U.S. Navy is one of the mightiest weapons of war ever seen on the planet. At the Navy's apex are its carrier groups, which can project war-winning power across the globe with unequalled speed. The Navy's compliment of submarines form the stealthiest element of the nation's strategic triad, capable of cruising indefinitely and impacting targets across the globe. The Navy also includes more surgical capabilities, including its Brown Water contingent designed to operate on inland waterways, and SEAL teams that rank among the most elite forces in the world.

The modern Navy has the unique capability to operate at all levels of warfare, from strategic force projection, to anti-fleet defensive actions, to counterinsurgency operations, to anti-piracy measures. And the Navy's host of hospital and supply vessels make it one of the world's leaders in times of natural disasters and humanitarian crises.

OPPOSITE:
The Mailed Fist
An F/A-18-E Super Hornet prepares to launch from the aircraft carrier USS *Harry S. Truman* (CVN-75). In the 21st century, Navy carrier groups serve as one of the world's most potent weapons of war.

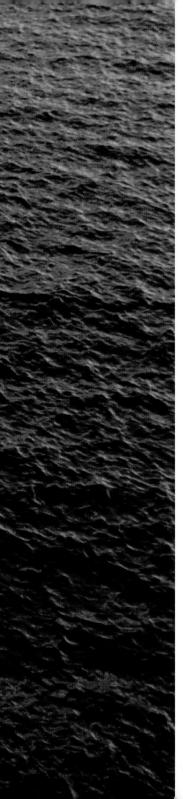

Firing a Salute

Firing squad members fire M-14 rifles for a 21-gun salute during a burial-at-sea ceremony for Aviation Electronics Technician 1st Class John P. Lamson aboard the aircraft carrier USS *George Washington* (CVN-73). The tradition of burial at sea aboard naval vessels dates as far back as the Greek triremes of ancient Athens. The tradition persisted through the age of sail, with the dead sewn into sail remnants before being consigned to the deep. Even aboard today's nuclear-powered vessels, naval tradition remains sacred.

RIGHT:

Celestial Reading, Atlantic Ocean, 2019

Quartermaster 2nd Class Javen Rogers uses a sextant to take a celestial reading from a weather deck aboard the aircraft carrier USS *John C. Stennis* (CVN-74). The sextant, invented by John Hadley in 1731, utilizes double reflection to measure angles between celestial objects and the horizon, allowing for accurate navigation while outside the sight of land. In the age of Global Positioning the Navy continues to hold its time-honored skills of seamanship dear.

LEFT AND TOP RIGHT:

Aircraft Maintenance

Pictured left, Aviation Machinist's Mate 3rd Class Ross Akersneff secures a jet engine to a carriage in the jet shop of the Nimitz-class aircraft carrier USS *Harry S. Truman* (CVN-75). Even amid the COVID-19 pandemic, the Navy must be ready for deployment at a moment's notice as part of OFRP, or the Optimized Fleet Response Plan. Maintaining Carrier Strike Groups, and their attendant airpower, is key to a nimble, worldwide naval capability.

Pictured right, Aviation Structural Mechanic Airman Apprentice Humberto Gonzalez works on an F/A-18E Super Hornet aboard the aircraft carrier USS *George H.W. Bush* (CVN-77). The carrier was deployed in the U.S. 5th Fleet area of operations in the volatile waters off of the Middle East. Supporting maritime security operations designed to reassure allies and partners remains a key strategic goal in the 21st century.

BOTTOM RIGHT:

Standing Watch

Boatswain's Mate Seaman Oscar Agujio stands watch aboard the aircraft carrier USS *Dwight D. Eisenhower* (CVN-69) on its 2020 Atlantic cruise. With near-peer competitor navies, especially those of Russia and China, on the rise, vigilance is key to naval survival.

Stanchion Barricade
Sailors prepare to stow netting for a stanchion barricade during flight deck drills aboard the aircraft carrier USS *John C. Stennis* (CVN-74) in the Atlantic Ocean, 2019. Carriers normally use arrestor gear to slow landing aircraft to a safe speed. However, if the tailhook of the landing aircraft is damaged, or if the aircraft has no tail hook, the last line of defense is the stanchion barricade—a durable netting raised in times of landing emergency.

LEFT:

Presenting the Navy Story
Mass Communication
Specialist 1st Class Shannon
E. Renfroe takes photos
during fleet operations
in the Pacific Ocean. The
21st century Navy is at the
forefront of change in both
gender and racial equality in
the U.S. military. The Navy
also leads the way in adapting
to the new realms of social
media and public outreach.

OPPOSITE:

Making Repairs
A Hull Maintenance
Technician makes repairs
aboard the aircraft carrier
USS *Gerald R. Ford* (CVN-
78). The Navy has had a
long history of conducting
needed repairs and upgrades,
even while on operations.
What once meant repairing
sails, weaving new ropes, and
hewing spars now means a
host of technical operations
undertaken by modern
systems specialists.

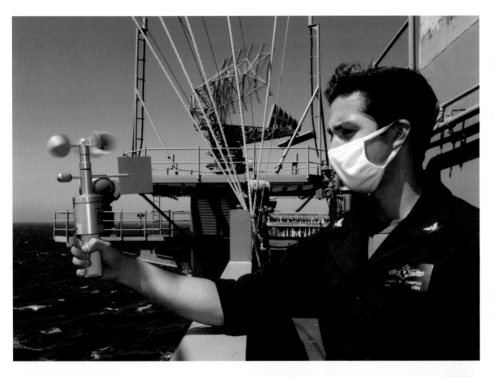

TOP LEFT:

Weather Forecasting

Aerographer's Mate 3rd Class Daniel Campos using a handheld anemometer aboard the aircraft carrier USS *Abraham Lincoln* (CVN-72). Accurate weather forecasting has always been central to successful naval operations. Aerographer's Mates aboard carriers and cruisers combine local observations, radar, and satellite information to create accurate micro forecasts that give the Navy a critical edge.

BELOW LEFT:

Cleaning the Bulkhead

Logistics Specialist 2nd Class Kenya Crenshaw cleans the bulkhead during a freshwater wash down. Dating back to the earliest wooden vessels of Greece and China, routine ship maintenance, from swabbing the deck to tarring joints, was an indispensable part of seagoing life. Even in the 21st century Navy mundane matters of upkeep are key to the operational lifespan of vessels.

ABOVE:

Replenishment at Sea

Tiffany Whaley communicates with the Military Sealift Command ship USNS *John Lenthall* (T-AO-189). Navies used to rely on a series of coaling stations dotted around the globe for docking and replenishing supplies while on operations. Navies now use the Standard Tensioned Replenishment Alongside Method, which involves connecting the ships with cables and pipelines.

PREVIOUS PAGE:
Rigid-Hull Inflatable Boat
Sailors lower a rigid-hull inflatable boat from the aircraft carrier USS *John C. Stennis* (CVN-74). Rigid-hull inflatable boats allow for quick usage and storage for a variety of important missions, including search and rescue for downed pilots or lost crew, the ferrying of personnel and equipment, and even force projection in waters congested with smaller craft.

ABOVE:
Underwater Explosive Ordnance Training
An explosive ordnance disposal technician conducts underwater training. The training took place in an onshore facility at Naval Support Activity Bahrain, demonstrating the ongoing commitment of U.S. naval forces in the volatile Middle East. In a world of asymmetric warfare at sea, the widespread use of explosive ordinance, a seaborne version of the infamous improvised explosive device (IED), is an ever-growing concern.

RIGHT:
Washing Down an F/A-18F Super Hornet
Captain Ana Tavira washes down an F/A-18F Super Hornet aircraft. Maintaining aircraft aboard the Navy's carriers amid salt spray and often brutal weather conditions is a round-the-clock task. Any number of things can go wrong with the delicate flight and weapons systems.

OPPOSITE:
Inshore Boat Unit (IBU) Exercises
Sailors participate in the joint command exercise Seahawk 2006 in San Diego, California. The exercise includes port clearance, shore patrols, security assistance, and improvised explosive device (IED) training.

USS *Carl Vinson*

The aircraft carrier USS *Carl Vinson* (CVN-70) on operations in the Pacific. Powered by two Westinghouse A4W nuclear reactors, the *Carl Vinson* can cruise at 30 knots and has an unlimited range. With a crew of over 6,000 and carrying 90 fixed-wing aircraft and helicopters, the supercarrier is one of the mightiest weapons of war ever built.

OPPOSITE:

The "Shooter"

The "shooter" signals to an F/A-18E Super Hornet on the flight deck of the USS *Ronald Reagan* (CVN-76). Launching and retrieving aircraft aboard a Navy carrier is a minutely-choreographed ballet, where anything could go wrong.

Among those leading the symphony are the plane directors and aircraft handling officers—universally known as the

"Yellow Shirts," who conduct the launches and retrievals via a system of hand signals, often delivered with great gusto. The Yellow Shirt tasked with the final launch is known as the "Shooter."

LEFT:

Steam Catapult

The flight deck aboard U.S. carriers is a rainbow of color. The "Green Shirts" include the important positions of catapult and arresting gear crew. While Electromagnetic Aircraft Launch Systems are presently in development, most older U.S. carriers still rely on steam catapults to propel heavy aircraft to launch speeds in a very limited space. The steam, diverted from the ship's mighty boilers, billows up around this "Green Shirt," following a take-off.

ABOVE:

The Blue Angels

Lead solo pilot Lieutenant Commander (LCDR) Brandon Hempler of the U.S. Navy Flight Demonstration Squadron, the Blue Angels, climbs dramatically in an F/A-18A Hornet. The Blue Angels were formed in 1946 and are the second oldest aerobatic flying team in the world. Specialists in precision formation flying and aerobatic stunts, they have performed for an estimated 11 million spectators every year, and are a staple of patriotic events from coast to coast.

LEFT:

Engine Maintenance

Gas Turbine Systems Technician 3rd Class Cleothy Smith takes a fuel sample. Electrical and mechanical technicians work to maintain a wide variety of gas turbine engines and propulsion control systems aboard ships of the fleet after 22 weeks of dedicated training at the Great Lakes Naval Training Center outside Chicago.

OPPOSITE:

Firefighter Training

Sailors test a P-25 firefighting truck aboard the amphibious assault ship USS *Iwo Jima* (LHD-7). Amphibious assault ships of this class are designed to support amphibious landing craft and also often house fixed-wing aircraft or helicopters designed to support forces ashore. Given their dangerous proximity between the battles of shore and sea, the "Red Shirts" of such craft (firefighters and damage control parties) must always be at the peak of training.

OPPOSITE:
**Fast Attack Submarine
USS *Alexandria* (SSN-757)**
Surfacing through the ice
near the North Pole, the
Alexandria demonstrates
the flexibility of the Navy's
submarine force. Armed
with torpedoes, anti ship
missiles, and Tomahawk
cruise missiles, the fast attack
submarines can stealthily
bring deadly force to bear
both at sea and on land.

RIGHT:
Graduation Ceremony
The recruit ceremonial honor
guard stands at parade rest
during a pass-in-review
graduation ceremony inside
Midway Ceremonial Drill
Hall at Recruit Training
Command, Chicago. More
than 30,000 recruits graduate
annually from the Navy's only
boot camp.

Origins
to World War I

The Navy's origins date back to 1775 when the Continental Congress authorized the purchase of two vessels to operate against British merchant shipping. American ships harassed British shipping, raided the British coast, and even won victories against British warships. But after the conflict had ended, Congress sold off the last ship, and the Continental Navy was disbanded. Without a major naval force, American shipping fell prey to piracy, especially off the coast of North Africa, and in the Naval Act of 1794 the Navy was back to stay, purchasing six frigates, including the USS *United States*, USS *Constellation*, and USS *Constitution*. The Navy quickly proved its worth as an instrument of power projection in the Second Barbary War, the landing of troops during the Mexican-American War, and with Commodore Matthew Perry's opening of trade with Japan.

During the Civil War, the Navy played a crucial role through establishing and then maintaining a blockade on the Confederacy and in severing the Confederacy's inland trade and communications in riverine operations. Most famous, perhaps, was the Civil War's advent of ironclad ships with the clash of the USS *Monitor* and the CSS *Virginia*, which forever altered the nature of war at sea. It was entry into World War I, though, that pressed the U.S. Navy into a true place on the world's maritime stage. With the shift to Dreadnoughts, oil-powered all big-gun battleships, and the threat posed by German U-Boats, the Navy became a much more dominant part of America's plans for both defense and force projection as presidents from Woodrow Wilson to Franklin Roosevelt sought to increase America's role as a major player in the world's power politics. As the age of naval airpower neared, the Navy was poised to take a place of world dominance.

OPPOSITE:
Bonhomme Richard in battle with HMS *Serapis*
Having gained acclaim during the American Revolution for daring raids on the English coast, Captain John Paul Jones took a tiny squadron into the North Sea seeking prey. On September 23, 1789 he joined battle with the HMS *Serapis*. Badly outgunned, the situation for the Americans was dire, and the commander of *Serapis* asked for Jones' surrender. Jones replied, "Surrender be damned! I have not yet begun to fight!" Shortly thereafter an explosion rocked the *Serapis'* arms magazines, forcing the British to surrender and providing the fledgling Continental Navy with a resounding victory.

LEFT:

Lieutenant Stephen Decatur and Midshipman Thomas Macdonough Boarding a Tripolitan Gun Boat, First Barbary War

In response to repeated piracy of its vessels in the Mediterranean, the young republic declared war on the Barbary States of North Africa. During a series of confused battles in Tripoli Harbor, Lieutenant Decatur's brother was mortally wounded by a Barbary pirate who was feigning surrender. Decatur took his gunboat and attacked the Barbary vessel, even though they were outnumbered 5-1. After an epic struggle, Decatur dispatched the pirate captain with a pistol shot at point blank range. His actions gave the Navy one of its first great heroes, and with the war's end in 1805 the Navy had its first great victory as a nation.

RIGHT:

Death of Captain Lawrence

During the War of 1812 Captain Vere Broke of the blockading British frigate *Shannon* sent a note challenging Captain James Lawrence of the American frigate *Chesapeake* to a single-ship duel. On June 1, 1813, the ships met in a high casualty battle near Boston. Lawrence was mortally wounded as he commanded from the deck of the *Chesapeake*, and gave his last command: "Don't give up the ship."

LEFT:

Commodore Perry's Expedition to Japan, July 14, 1853
With Japan isolated and refusing almost all contact with foreigners while the western powers jostled for trade dominance in the Pacific, the U.S. dispatched a fleet under Commodore Matthew Perry to force open Japan to U.S. trade. Perry first arrived at Japan's capital of Edo in July, announcing his coming with blank fire from 73 cannon. Followed by a second visit in 1854 in which Perry threatened war, the Japanese signed the Convention of Kanagawa, allowing for U.S. trade.

ABOVE:

Battle of Mobile Bay, August 1864
Seeking to seize the Confederate port of Mobile and complete the Union blockade during the Civil War, Admiral David Farragut had already lost a ship to a Confederate minefield. Seeing victory in sight against the smaller Confederate fleet under Admiral Franklin Buchanan, Farragut yelled: "Damn the torpedoes! Full steam ahead!" Farragut then destroyed the Confederate fleet, including the ironclad *Tennessee*, and captured the three forts that guarded the port.

RIGHT:
USS *Monitor*

Having received intelligence
that the Confederate Navy
was commissioning an
ironclad warship, *Virginia*,
the Union hurried to counter
with the construction of
the USS *Monitor*. The first
ironclad in the Navy, *Monitor*
boasted a revolving turret and
the radical design of John
Ericsson. Rushed into action,
Monitor met *Virginia* in battle
at Hampton Roads in March
1862, and the first battle
between ironclads ensued.
The struggle lasted more
than four hours, with neither
ship able to gain the upper
hand or cause damage to the
other. The age of the ironclads
had begun.

OPPOSITE:
USS *Canonicus*

The launch of the USS
Monitor had touched off
a flurry of production,
eventually numbering 84
ironclads in the Union Navy,
64 of which were the *Monitor*
type. Some were river service
ships, while others, including
the Canonicus class, were
meant for ocean service.
While searching for the
Confederate ironclad
Stonewall, the *Canonicus*
was sent to Havana, Cuba,
making it the first Navy
ironclad to visit a foreign port.

"THE SWORD IS DRAWN THE NAVY UPHOLDS IT!"

WE CAN DO NO OTHERWISE

U.S. NAVY RECRUITING STATION

34 East 23rd Street
New York

LEFT:
World War I Naval Recruiting Poster
U.S. entry into World War I in April 1917 called for an unprecedented expansion on the part of the Navy to face the German threat. The eightfold increase in fleet power resulted in a Navy of 645 ships by the war's end, with an additional 563 ships under construction.

ABOVE:
Gunners on Board the battleship USS *New York* Load a 5-inch Gun
The *New York* class of battleships began to enter service in the Navy in 1914 as part of an effort to upgun the Navy. The *New York* was the first Navy vessel to mount 14-inch main guns, which could fire a 1400lb armor-piercing shell 13 miles (21 km).

OPPOSITE:
Yeomanettes, 1918
As part of the naval expansion in the run up to World War I, Secretary of the Navy Josephus Daniels sought the inclusion of women. Loretta Perfectus Walsh became the first female to serve in the Navy, when she joined the Naval Reserve in March 1917. Eventually more than 11,000 women joined the Navy during the war.

LEFT:

USS *Christabel*

A civilian yacht purchased by the Navy and refitted with 3-inch guns and depth charges for anti-submarine patrol duty in World War I. On May 18, 1918, *Christabel* twice sighted and engaged German submarine UC-56. After dropping depth charges, debris rose to the surface, indicating the demise of the U-Boat, resulting in the honor of a white star painted on *Christabel*'s smokestack.

TOP RIGHT:

USS *George Washington* Arrives in New York Harbor, Greeted by President Woodrow Wilson

The ship had been built in 1912 for a German shipping company and was capable of carrying 3,000 passengers. Seized by the U.S. upon entry of the war, the ship was employed as a troop transport, making its first voyage in December 1917. By the end of the war, the USS *George Washington* had carried 48,000 troops to France.

BOTTOM RIGHT:

USS *Langley* (CV-1)

The *Langley* was the Navy's first aircraft carrier, converted in 1920 from the collier USS *Jupiter*. The *Langley* saw service in World War II as a seaplane tender, and was hit by Japanese bombers in 1942. She was damaged so badly that she had to be scuttled.

Black Mess Attendants, USS *Bushnell*

African-Americans had served in the Navy since the Revolution, in an integrated setting. During the War of 1812, blacks comprised nearly 20 percent of the Navy's manpower, a percentage equaled in the Civil War. The situation worsened during the early 20th century, with segregation becoming the norm and with African-Americans often relegated to service as mess attendants.

LEFT:

**Boxing Instruction,
Naval Training Station,
San Francisco**
Since its foundation, the
Navy has involved sporting
competitions of all types,
with "smokers" being
arranged between individual
ships that often revolved
around boxing matches.

RIGHT:

**USS *Illinois* (BB-7), Algiers,
Louisiana**
As the Navy grew and its ships
became ever larger, modern
repair facilities were a must.
An act of Congress in 1898
approved the funding of a
massive new drydock outside
New Orleans. The huge
structure was completed by
1901, and its lift capacity
of 18,000 tons made it the
largest in the world. Its first
"customer" was the battleship
USS *Illinois*.

Main Guns, USS *Florida* (BB-30)
One of the Navy's first dreadnought class battleships, the USS
Florida boasted a main battery of ten 12-inch guns. USS *Florida*
was sent to reinforce the British Grand Fleet during World
War I, conducting fleet patrols in the North Sea and guarding
convoys to Norway.

USS *Wyoming* Leading a Naval Column
With her main battery of twelve 12-inch guns, USS *Wyoming*
joined USS *Florida* attached to the British Grand Fleet in the
North Sea during World War I. During the disarmament prior
to World War II, USS *Wyoming* was converted into a training
ship, training 35,000 gunners for the upcoming conflict.

U.S.S. BIRMINGHAM

OPPOSITE:
USS *Birmingham*
Civilian pilot Eugene Ely made the first ever aircraft takeoff from the USS *Birmingham* in 1910 in his Curtiss Model D biplane. In June 1917 USS *Birmingham* escorted the first ever U.S. troop convoy to France, and remained on convoy duty for the remainder of the war.

ABOVE:
Coal Heavers and Passers
World War I saw a monumental shift from coal-fired boilers to oil. Traditional coal-fired boilers could consume 8–12 tons of coal per hour, and the last Navy coal-fired warship, the USS *Texas* launched in 1916, carried 124,000 cubic feet (3511 cubic meters) of coal. The USS *Nevada*, launched in 1914, was the first U.S. battleship to burn oil, which produced far more energy per pound than coal.

OPPOSITE:

Loading a Torpedo Aboard the USS *K-5* Submarine
Submarines altered warfare during World War I as weapons against merchant shipping and against warships. *K-5*, launched in 1914, was the first U.S. submarine to operate in European waters in World War I, serving out of the Azores searching for enemy U-boats and surface raiders.

LEFT:

***O-11* (SS-72) Fitting Out at the Lake Torpedo Boat Co., Bridgeport, Connecticut**
Introduced in 1917, the O class of submarines were larger and more fitted to ocean voyages than their predecessors. Most served in an anti-submarine role off of the American east coast. Two O class submarines came under fire from a British merchantman, which mistook them for U-boats.

LEFT:

USS *Alabama* (BB-8)
A pre-dreadnought battleship armed with a main battery of four 13-inch guns, the ship served in a training role during World War I. After the war, in 1921, the USS *Alabama* was bombed by aircraft of the U.S. Army Air Service under the supervision of General Billy Mitchell. A series of three tests succeeded in sinking the unmanned and stationary vessel, leading to Mitchell championing the power of the bomber over the Navy.

RIGHT:

Wheelhouse of the USS *Bainbridge*
A destroyer launched in 1920. While on operations in the Mediterranean Sea, the USS *Bainbridge* assisted in a humanitarian evacuation of Armenian civilians from the Great Fire of Smyrna in Turkey. The fire was part of the notorious Armenian genocide, with the Great Fire alone killing nearly 100,000.

LEFT:

U.S. Navy Seaplane at Norfolk, Virginia, 1930
The advent of airpower was transformative for navies between the wars. Fleets across the world had to deal with projecting air power and defending against the same. Seaplanes, capable of water landings, could launch from capital ships and were critical in a reconnaissance role. But the attack role would fall to the new aircraft carriers.

OPPOSITE:

USS *Shenandoah* (ZR-1)
Designed for fleet reconnaissance, *Shenandoah* was launched in 1923. Provided lift by 2,100,000 cubic feet (59,465 cubic meters) of helium, *Shenandoah* successfully made the first crossing of North America by airship. However, on its 57th flight in 1925, a violent updraft during a storm pushed it higher than its pressure limits, where it was ripped apart. Airships were not the answer for naval air power.

RIGHT:

Sailors Scrubbing the Deck, USS _Pennsylvania_

Launched in 1915, USS _Pennsylvania_ was a super dreadnought battleship, boasting twelve 14-inch guns and powered by an oil-burning propulsion system. She did not accompany other U.S. battleships to Europe due to the lack of fuel oil. In 1918, USS _Pennsylvania_ escorted President Woodrow Wilson to France for the peace talks at Versailles.

After the war, she served as flagship of the Atlantic Fleet and was present at Pearl Harbor for the outbreak of World War II.

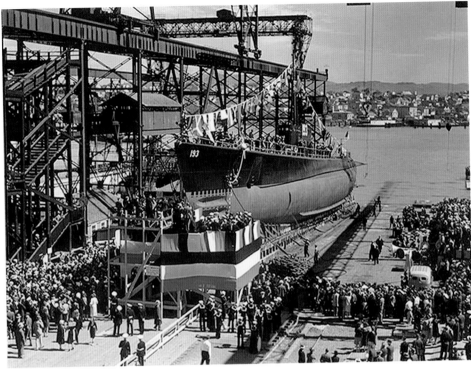

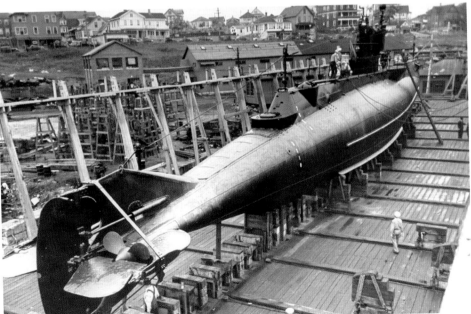

ABOVE LEFT:
Cooks, USS *Brooklyn*, 1938
Keeping a crew of over a thousand men fed around the clock was a daunting task. When on operations, diets of the sailors depended on when refrigerated resupply ships arrived. After restocking, the sailors enjoyed beef for several days, but then it was back to dehydrated rations that required the touch of a deft cook, and, of course SPAM.

LEFT:
USS *R-14* (SS-91)
Launched in 1919, *R-14* operated out of Pearl Harbor. While on a patrol to locate a lost tug, *R-14* ran out of fuel and lost radio communications. The ship's engineering officer developed a novel solution – using bunks lashed together and the torpedo loading crane for support, sails were constructed out of blankets and hammocks. After sailing for 64 hours, *R-14* safely returned to port.

ABOVE:
USS *Swordfish* (SS-193)
A Sargo class submarine, the *Swordfish* was a significant step forward with a range of 11,000 nautical miles, which allowed for operations in Japanese home waters. Stationed in the Philippines, the *Swordfish* reached Japan shortly after Pearl Harbor and, on December 16, 1941, was the first American submarine to sink a Japanese vessel, the cargo ship *Atsutasan Maru*. *Swordfish* was lost to Japanese attack in 1945.

World War II

The Navy faced an unprecedented series of challenges in World War II—the threat of the powerful Imperial Japanese Navy in the Pacific, predation by German U-Boat "wolfpacks" in the Battle of the Atlantic, clashes at sea from the Indian Ocean to the Antarctic, transporting entire armies across the Pacific Ocean and the Atlantic, and then having to implement invasions from North Africa to Sicily to France, to the Solomon Islands, to the Gilberts, to Japan itself.

Casting off the interwar restrictions on naval building programs, the Navy expanded at an astounding rate as it found itself at the center of U.S strategy in a two-ocean war. In the Pacific, the Navy fought six great battles with the Japanese: Pearl Harbor, Coral Sea, Midway, Philippine Sea, Leyte Gulf, and Okinawa. In the Pacific Theater, the Navy undertook more than 100 amphibious landings against Japanese targets. In the Atlantic, destroyers and escort carriers fought a brutal campaign against German U-Boats, making the Battle of the Atlantic the longest single battle of the entire war and a crushing victory in which the Germans lost more than 700 submarines and suffered a 75 percent casualty rate among U-Boat crews. Operations Torch, Husky, and Overlord were important naval successes in landing massive forces against hardened defenses—operations in which the Navy changed the course of the war. By the end of the war the Navy had far supplanted the British Royal Navy as the leading naval force in the world, totaling an astounding 70 percent of the world's naval tonnage. The Navy was now the dominant force on the planet.

OPPOSITE:
A Patrol Torpedo (PT) Boat Fires
a 20mm Anti-Aircraft Machine Gun
World War II would prove the sternest ever test for the Navy, which fought a global, multi-ocean series of campaigns. By war's end the Navy counted 6,768 warships, including at its pinnacle 28 fleet aircraft carriers and 71 escort carriers, down to 1,204 nimble PT Boats.

OPPOSITE:

USS *West Virginia* (BB-48) Aflame at Pearl Harbor

On December 7, 1941, Japanese carrier aircraft struck the U.S. Pacific Fleet in a surprise attack, sinking four battleships, damaging four others, and sinking or damaging 11 other cruisers and destroyers. However, it had not been the knockout blow that the Japanese had hoped for, since none of the Pacific Fleet's aircraft carriers were in Pearl Harbor at the time of attack.

RIGHT:

U.S. Sailors Pay Tribute to Pearl Harbor Victims, Naval Air Station Kaneohe Bay

During the Japanese surprise attack on Pearl Harbor, masterminded by Admiral Isoroku Yamamoto, 2,403 Americans were killed and 1,178 wounded. Yamamoto had hoped that America would be too fractured to rise to the challenge of a devastating war. Instead, Pearl Harbor galvanized the American public like never before, and became a "Day that will live in infamy."

SBD-3 Dauntless and F4F-4 Wildcat Fighters, USS *Santee* (ACV-29)
The Wildcat was the most effective Navy fighter at the beginning of World War II. Although slower than the famed Japanese Zero, the Wildcat made up for its shortcomings with its ruggedness in operations. Its kill to loss ratio for the war stood at nearly 7-1.

PBY Catalina Loaded with 500lb bombs, Midway Island

With a range of over 2,000 miles (3,200 km) and with water landing capabilities, the Catalina was one of the outstanding patrol aircraft of the Pacific War. On June 3, 1942, it was a Catalina that first sighted Japanese transport ships 700 miles (1,120 km) west of Midway. The next morning another Catalina made first contact with the Japanese carrier group, radioing the carriers' location to the U.S. fleet.

USS _Yorktown_ (CV-5) at Midway
After launching a devastating strike on the Japanese carrier force, _Yorktown_ was discovered by aircraft from the surviving Japanese carrier _Hiryu_. Hits by five bombs knocked out _Yorktown_'s boilers. Across the giant's decks, repair workers scrambled to keep the ship afloat. An hour later, though, a second wave struck _Yorktown_ with two torpedoes, causing a loss of all power and a list of 23 degrees.

ABOVE:
Torpedo Squadron Six (VT-6), USS *Enterprise* (CV-6) at Midway
The Torpedo Dive Bomber (TBD) Devastators were slow and its torpedoes unreliable. Having lost contact with their fighter escort, the TBDs were the first to arrive above the Japanese carrier force and attacked unescorted. VT-6 lost nine of its 14 TBDs, while VT-3 from *Yorktown* lost 10 of its 12 Devastators. Even though the TBDs had failed to score any hits against the Japanese carriers, they diverted the attention of defending Japanese aircraft from an incoming flight of Dauntless dive bombers that turned the tide of battle.

TOP RIGHT:
USS *Astoria* (CA-34) steams by USS *Yorktown* (CV-5)
Although crippled by Japanese bombs, the *Yorktown* fought on. VB-3, a flight of Dauntless dive bombers from *Yorktown*, pummeled Japanese aircraft carrier *Soryu*, scoring three direct hits that ignited aircraft fuel and cooked off piles of stacked ammunition. Unable to land on *Yorktown*, the orphaned aircraft landed on USS *Enterprise* and USS *Hornet*, while *Soryu* sunk, along with three other Japanese carriers.

BELOW RIGHT:
USS *Yorktown* (CV-5) Burning During the Battle of Midway
After being crippled in the Battle of the Coral Sea, *Yorktown* had barely made it to Midway, with repairs continuing even as the ship made its way into battle. After being struck by both bombs and torpedoes, it seemed that *Yorktown*, against all odds, would once again survive and she was taken under tow. On the afternoon of June 6, 1942, she was struck by torpedoes from a Japanese submarine. It was the next day before the mighty ship slid beneath the waves.

OPPOSITE:

Invasion Convoy, Morocco, November 1942

The first major invasion in the European Theater was in North Africa and was dubbed Operation Torch. The firepower and transport ability of the Navy made the operations possible, giving operations on land nearly unlimited flexibility and a critical edge.

LEFT:

Admiral Chester W. Nimitz Pins the Navy Cross on Doris "Dorie" Miller

A Steward's Mate, Miller had just served breakfast on the USS *West Virginia* when the attack began at Pearl Harbor. He rushed into action, taking the controls of a .50 caliber anti-aircraft machine gun. For his bravery, Miller was the first black American to receive the Navy Cross.

ABOVE:

Pistol Shooting Practice, U.S. Naval Academy

With the demand for naval officers at an all-time high, the Naval Academy began to graduate midshipmen in three years rather than the customary four. The Academy also began its reserve officer school, and by the end of the conflict, 10 classes of reserve midshipmen had graduated, totaling 3,319.

LEFT:

Navy Hospital Ship USS *Solace* (AH-5)

Commissioned in August 1941, the *Solace* was in Pearl Harbor on December 7, 1941, rescuing badly burned sailors from both USS *Arizona* and *Oklahoma*. With a capacity of 418 patients and a crew of 466, the *Solace* served with distinction in operations across the Pacific Theater, earning seven battle stars. Often jam-packed with over 500 patients, *Solace* cared for soldiers and sailors fresh from the battlefields and transported them to medical facilities from Australia to Pearl Harbor.

OPPOSITE:

Medical Personnel Carrying Wounded, USS *Solace*

With the far-flung nature of the Pacific War often being fought on remote islands far from advanced medical care, ships like *Solace* were in high demand. On tiny islands from Tarawa to Kwajalein Atoll, medical care was often limited to battlefield medics. Only arrival on the *Solace* and her sister ships afforded the life-saving care needed for the badly wounded.

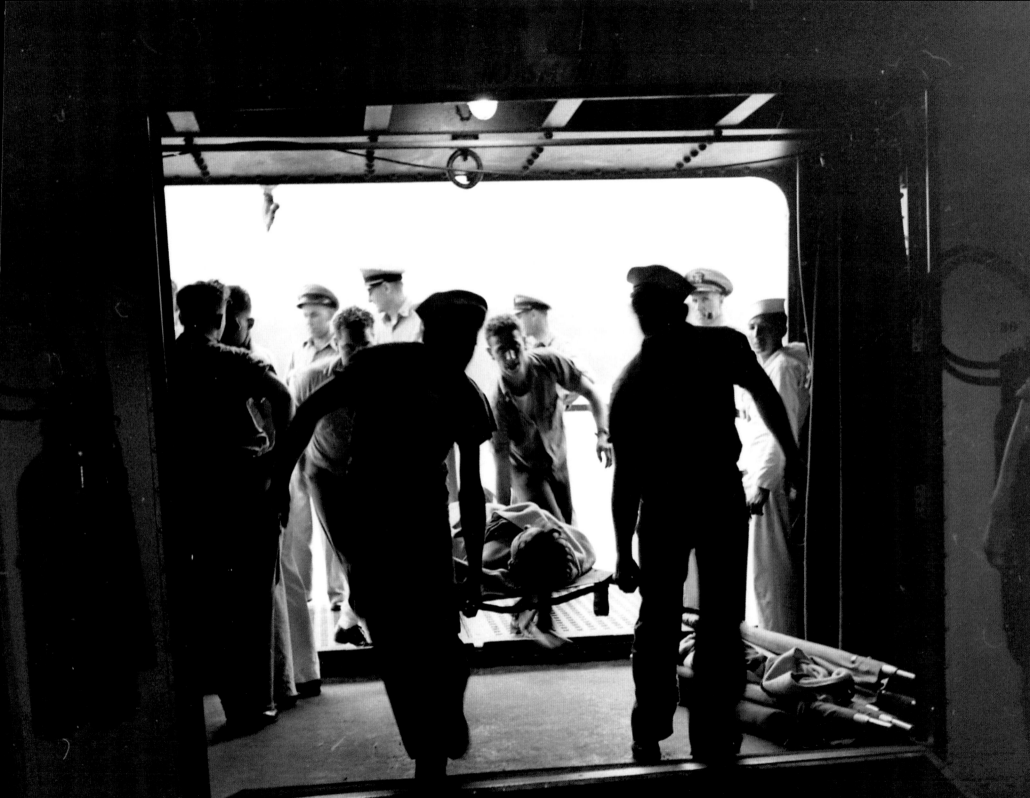

Sailors Practice Lifeboat Drills, USS *Doran* (DD-634)
The destroyer *Doran* took part in the crucial Atlantic convoys to Britain and North Africa that kept critical supplies and manpower flowing to the Allied war effort in Europe. Nimble destroyers were a key part of the convoy effort. During the Battle of the Atlantic, over 60,000 Allied Navy and merchant sailors were lost.

FAR LEFT:

Navy Signalmen

Signals intelligence are often key to winning wars. A joint Army–Navy program in the Pacific dubbed "Magic" often succeeded in breaking Japanese codes, especially those of its diplomatic corps sent over a system known as Purple.

TOP RIGHT:

Naval Construction Battalion Train as Seabees

In 1940 only 2.3 percent of naval personnel were black, with most serving as stewards and messmen. During World War II three all-black Seabee battalions were formed. Their motto was "proving our worth." In these segregated battalions a total of 12,500 African-Americans served, building advanced bases and breaking institutional concepts of race in the Navy.

BOTTOM RIGHT:

Convoy PQ-17 Gathers Outside Hvalfjord, Iceland

Part of the dangerous convoy route from Iceland to Archangelsk in the USSR, the ships escorting PQ-17 received intelligence that German surface vessels, including the battleship *Tirpitz*, were on an intercept course. The joint British-American escort force, including USS *Washington* (BB-56), were ordered to intercept the Germans and the convoy instructed to scatter. Attacked by German aircraft and submarines, 24 of the 35 merchant ships were sunk.

**Crewmen Receive Mail,
USS *Argonaut* (SM-1)**
Argonaut, along with
Nautilus, transported 200
Marine raiders to Makin
Island in August 1942. The
Makin Raid was the first U.S.
ground offensive in the Pacific,
and involved landing Marines
on Makin via rubber boats.

OPPOSITE:
**USS *Argonaut* (SM-1)
Docks at Pearl Harbor**
After their successful raid,
72 Marines were stranded on
Makin by heavy surf.
The Marines fashioned a raft
and made it to sea, but 11
were missing in action. Nine
were captured and executed
by Japanese forces. The
remaining two have never
been accounted for.

OPPOSITE:
USS *Hornet* (CV-8)
Veteran of the Doolittle Raid and the Battle of Midway, in August 1942 *Hornet* made its way to the Solomon Islands off Guadalcanal. It was the first major ground offensive by U.S. forces, and the Japanese reacted with fury, resulting in seven major naval clashes, in which 29 U.S. ships were sunk. In October 1942 *Hornet* and *Enterprise* intercepted a Japanese force in the Battle of the Santa Cruz Islands. During the fighting *Hornet* was hit by both bombs and torpedoes and by two Japanese aircraft. After some repair work, *Hornet* was struck again by another torpedo. Fearing the approach of the Japanese fleet, Vice Admiral William Halsey ordered *Hornet* sunk. Nine torpedoes and 400 rounds of fire from destroyers failed to complete the task. Japanese destroyers finally finished the task by firing 24 torpedoes.

LEFT:
Landing Craft Mechanized (LCM), Operation "Husky"
The landings on the beaches of Sicily were the largest of the war, extensively utilizing the Navy's flat-bottomed landing craft. The versatility of these craft allowed not only for beach landings, but for beach resupply efforts. Their successes in Sicily proved to Allied planners that the coming invasion of Normandy could be accomplished without capturing a port.

OPPOSITE FAR LEFT:

USS *Hornet* (CV-12)

The Navy wasn't without an aircraft carrier named *Hornet* for long. After the loss of the Yorktown-class *Hornet* in October of 1942, a new Essex-class USS *Hornet* was ready for operations a year later. Able to carry 100 aircraft into battle, the new carrier packed a considerable punch.

OPPOSITE ABOVE RIGHT:

Personnel Inspection Aboard USS *Biloxi* (CL-80)

Also launched during the naval buildup of 1943, the Cleveland-class light cruiser hurried to the Pacific Theater to take part in operations to neutralize the Japanese base at Truk. *Biloxi* was equipped with floatplanes for spotting and rescue missions.

OPPOSITE BELOW RIGHT:

Pilots Prepare for Takeoff, USS *Lexington* (CV-16)

Renamed in honor of the aircraft carrier *Lexington* lost in the Battle of the Coral Sea, the new Essex-class *Lexington* became known as the Blue Ghost to the Japanese, who were surprised that she had returned. In December 1943 *Lexington* was struck by torpedoes off Kwajalein and the Japanese again reported her sunk. After repairs, *Lexington* was back for more, only to be reported sunk by the Japanese again in the Battle of Leyte Gulf. But to the dismay of the Japanese, the Blue Ghost still fought on.

PREVIOUS PAGE:
**Coast Guardsmen Watch
a Depth Charge Detonate**
By 1943 the Battle of the
Atlantic was reaching its
peak, with the Germans
having perfected "wolfpack"
tactics, as the Navy countered
with more convoy escorts
and advanced depth charges.
After the explosion of a
depth charge, the German
U-Boat surfaced, where it was
destroyed by naval gunfire.
During "Black May" alone the
Germans lost 43 submarines
destroyed and 37 damaged,
forcing them to call off
operations in the Atlantic.

RIGHT:

**U.S. Troops Board LSTs
(Landing Ships Tank) for
Operation Dragoon**
After the success of the
Normandy invasion, Allied
forces also invaded southern
France in Operation
Dragoon (August 1944). The
unparalleled versatility of flat-
bottomed landing craft opened
opportunities across the
European theater, including
the Operation Shingle landings
at Anzio in Italy.

OPPOSITE:

**Landing Craft Infantry
(Large), Normandy Invasion**
The naval portion of the
D-Day landings in June 1944
was Operation Neptune,
which involved an astounding
6,939 vessels, including 1,213
warships, 4,126 landing craft,
736 ancillary craft, and 864
merchant vessels.

USS *Idaho*

American battleship USS *Idaho* (BB-42) ploughs through the Pacific Ocean during the operation to capture the Marshall Islands, January–February 1944. *Idaho* was part of the bombardment group for the invasions of the islands of Iwo Jima and Okinawa in 1945, and suffered damage from a Japanese *kamikaze* attack during the latter campaign.

LEFT:

Plane Handlers Rest Aboard USS *Lexington* (CV-16), Battle of the Philippine Sea (June 19–20, 1944)

Responding to U.S. landings in the Marianas Islands, the Japanese attacked, resulting in the final carrier versus carrier battle of the Pacific War. The battle involved 15 U.S. carriers and 900 aircraft against nine Japanese carriers, 450 aircraft and 300 land-based aircraft. Japanese aircrew losses in previous battles left their pilots seriously outclassed and vulnerable, resulting in the "Great Marianas Turkey Shoot." The Navy lost 123 aircraft and no carriers, while the Japanese lost three carriers and 600 aircraft. The battle crushed Japanese carrier power in the Pacific.

RIGHT:

USS *Boise* (CL-47) Shelling the Coast of New Guinea

Fighting in the rugged terrain of New Guinea had been a difficult struggle for U.S. and Australian forces. As in campaigns on other islands in the Pacific, Navy firepower was always there to offer often overwhelming support. *Boise* alone could bring fifteen 6-inch (152mm) guns and eight 5-inch (127mm) guns to bear, enough to crush most enemy entrenchments day or night.

OPPOSITE:

USS *Bunker Hill* (CV-17) Hit by two Japanese *Kamikazes*, May 11, 1945

With the invasion of the home island of Okinawa, the Japanese became more desperate and unleashed nearly 1,500 *kamikazes* in Operation Kikusui. *Bunker Hill* was struck by *kamikazes* on the flight deck and near the island superstructure, killing 372 and wounding 264. The suicide attacks knocked 30 Navy ships out of action, but no aircraft carriers. *Bunker Hill* fought on.

LEFT:

40mm Anti-Aircraft Guns, USS *Hornet* (CV-12)
Defending against *kamikaze* attacks took iron nerve. The last line of defense was always the fleet's array of anti-aircraft guns, with some shells even armed with radio frequency proximity fuses that greatly increased accuracy.

ABOVE:

Five-inch Rockets Being Loaded Under the Wing of a Vought F4U Corsair
Entering service in large numbers by 1944, the Corsair quickly became a mainstay for the carrier fleet. Corsair pilots claimed 2,140 air combat victories against 189 losses. Even against the mighty

Japanese Zero the Corsair enjoyed a 12-1 kill ratio. Toward the end of the Pacific War, the Corsair saw more use in a ground-attack role.

LEFT:

**Japanese Surrender,
USS *Missouri* (BB-63)**
A veteran of the battles of
Iwo Jima and Okinawa,
Missouri was chosen as
the venue for the formal
Japanese surrender. General
Douglas MacArthur and
Japanese Foreign Minister
Mamoru Shigemitsu signed
the document on September
2, 1945, with the flag once
flown by Commodore
Matthew Perry when he
visited Japan in 1853
serving as a backdrop for
the occasion. The Navy's
greatest war ever had come
to a victorious conclusion.

From the Korean War to the Balkans

After its central role in the Allies' resounding victory in World War II, the United States adopted a stance of a global guardian against the aggression of the Soviet Union in the Cold War. As one of the two superpowers on the planet, the U.S. needed to project power on a global scale, a role tailor-made for the Navy—from the might of its carrier groups to the humanitarian aid provided by its hospital ships.

The postwar Navy was immediately put to the test with the Korean War, which called for the fleet to undertake operations that were not familiar in its repertoire, including the daring landings at Inchon. The advent of nuclear power made the Navy more versatile than ever, with its ships able to remain at sea or under the waves almost indefinitely. Nuclear power also presented a new threat, with the Navy demonstrating its versatility by enforcing a blockade on Cuba. When the Cold War again became hot in Vietnam, the Navy faced a dynamic tactical situation that looked to the future, while also hearkening back to the past. Navy carriers on Yankee and Dixie stations projected airpower into North Vietnam in a strategic role, and into South Vietnam in a troop support role. At the other end of the military spectrum, small brown water craft plied the endless waterways of the Mekong Delta in a counterinsurgency role in a riverine war that was reminiscent of actions in the American Civil War.

When the Cold War ended, American might was required in small conflicts from the Persian Gulf, to the Horn of Africa, to the Balkans. And, as always, the Navy stood ready as the optimal force to project U.S. power into the far corners of the world.

OPPOSITE:
USS *Coral Sea* (CVA-43)
The Catapult Officer signals launch and an A-4 Skyhawk starts down the flight deck, during operations in the South China Sea in 1965. The massive Cold War deployment against the Soviet Union went hot in far-flung and unexpected places. From the Korean peninsula, to Indochina, to the Balkans, the might of the Navy was critical to defending American interests in far away places around the globe.

Vought F-4U Corsair
Guarding the landing fleet, a Corsair circles above the harbor at Inchon in September 1950. With the Korean War hanging in the balance, General Douglas MacArthur opted for a daring amphibious landing behind enemy lines at Inchon. With the memories of the Navy's many D-Days in both Europe and the Pacific in World War II to guide him, MacArthur relied on naval know-how to turn the tide of America's newest war.

OPPOSITE:

Navy Landing Ships, Inchon, September 15th–19th, 1950
Four Landing Ship Tank craft (LSTs) unload men and equipment on the beach. The landing, dubbed Operation Chromite, involved 75,000 men and 261 naval vessels. With some of the strongest tides in the world barring their way, the Navy landed a reconnaissance team on a small island in the harbor, under Lieutenant Eugene Clark, who successfully charted the tides and discovered that the narrow channels were not guarded by enemy mines.

LEFT:

LCVPs Ready for the Invasion of Inchon

With the Navy having navigated the difficult tidal and tactical conditions at Inchon, the landing came as a devastating surprise to the North Korean People's Army. Having enjoyed an unstopped series of successes since the outbreak of the war, Inchon threw the North Koreans into a military tailspin. The South Korean capital of Seoul was recaptured within 10 days and within a month, 135,000 North Korean soldiers had become prisoners-of-war.

ABOVE:

USS *Missouri* (BB-63) Fires a Three-gun Salvo

Under the command of Vice Admiral Arthur Struble, a veteran of several amphibious operations in World War II, navy gunners dueled with North Korean coastal artillery to pave the way for the Inchon landings. Three Navy ships were struck by enemy fire, but the landing beaches were made secure.

OPPOSITE:

USS *Essex* (CV-9)
Navy aircraft were especially valuable in ground attack roles in Korea because of their ability to loiter over the battlefield due to the carriers' nearness. The USS *Essex* brought more firepower to bear than ever, being the first carrier to launch the F2H Banshee. On September 16, 1951, a Banshee that had been damaged crashed on landing, killing seven and destroying four aircraft.

RIGHT:

Snow Aboard the USS *Essex* (CV-9), 1952
Operating in the waters off of the Korean peninsula meant enduring weather conditions of all kinds, from searing heat in the summer to blinding snowstorms in the winter. In October 1952, Hurricane Ruth also barreled into the fleet area, causing a Navy troop transport to run aground and damaging several other ships, including the Australian aircraft carrier HMAS *Sydney*.

ABOVE:

USS *Nautilus* (SSN-571) is Greeted in New York Harbor

The *Nautilus* was the first nuclear submarine in the U.S. Navy. In 1958, leaving from Point Barrow, Alaska, *Nautilus* travelled 1,000 miles (1,600km) under the Arctic ice cap at a depth of 500 feet (152m), to accomplish the first undersea voyage to the North Pole.

OPPOSITE:

USS *Terrebonne Parish* (LST-1156) at Guantanamo Bay During the Cuban Missile Crisis, October 1962

Having detected Soviet-made nuclear missiles in Cuba, the Kennedy administration faced the Cold War turning hot 90 miles from the U.S. mainland. Any operations against the island nation, from an invasion to a blockade, would heavily involve naval power. Supporting the isolated U.S. base at Guantanamo Bay was also a naval mission. Such varied operations of the Cold War proved the worth of U.S. naval dominance.

LEFT:

USS *Vesole* Intercepting Missile-carrying Soviet Ship *Potzunov*, October 1962
At the height of the Cuban Missile Crisis President Kennedy declared a naval quarantine of Cuba, with Navy ships of all types tasked with barring any Soviet-allied ships carrying offensive weaponry, especially anything involved in the nuclear missile buildup. After a tense standoff, Soviet ships bound for Cuba turned back from the blockade, winning the U.S. a signature victory in the Cold War.

RIGHT:

U.S. Navy Swift Boats Patrolling the Saigon River
With much of the early stages of the Vietnam War taking the form of guerrilla actions, much of Navy involvement in the struggle would be through its brown-water force. In its biggest riverine war since the Civil War, Navy small craft performed a number of operations, including policing the vital port of Saigon against waterborne incursions by the Viet Cong.

LEFT:

USS *Franklin D. Roosevelt* (CVA-42), Gulf of Tonkin
Another major naval role during the Vietnam War was providing air support to ground troops in South Vietnam and against strategic targets in North Vietnam. Normally three carriers operated at Yankee Station in the Gulf of Tonkin against North Vietnamese targets, while a single carrier stood at Dixie Station off of Cam Ranh Bay to provide air support in South Vietnam.

OPPOSITE:

USS *Hancock* (CVA-19)
A crewman wheels a cart loaded with three Sidewinder air-to-air guided missiles across the flight deck during operations off Vietnam in April 1967. The main threat in operations in the skies above North Vietnam, especially to ground attack aircraft, was from anti-aircraft fire and from Soviet-supplied SA-2 and later SA-7 SAM missiles. There were also sorties by both MiG-17 and MiG-21 fighters, leading to dogfights in the skies above North Vietnam. There were two Navy aces of the Vietnam War, Randall "Duke" Cunningham and William Driscoll, both with five confirmed kills.

ABOVE:

A-7 Corsair II Prepares to Launch for a Mission over North Vietnam

A major target of naval aircraft in North Vietnam was transportation infrastructure. Bridges were notoriously difficult to hit, with the Than Hoa Bridge having survived several dedicated attacks. In 1972, Navy A-7s delivered two 2,000lb (907kg) Walleye television-guided bombs on target, permanently knocking out the bridge in an early use of "smart" weaponry.

ABOVE RIGHT:

Grumman A-6 Intruders

Entering service in 1963, the Intruder became the Navy's all-weather ground-attack aircraft of the Vietnam

War, capable of carrying an 18,000lb (8164kg) payload. Often flying low to attack enemy targets, the A-6 was vulnerable to ground fire, with 84 being lost during the conflict.

RIGHT:

A Navy UH-1 Launches a Rocket at a Viet Cong Target in the Mekong Delta

As the brown water commitment in the Mekong Delta grew in size, a need developed for a dedicated Navy attack helicopter squadron to support ground and riverine operations. In April 1967, HA(L)-3—dubbed the "Seawolves"—was activated. The Seawolves specialized in search and destroy, medevac missions,

and SEAL team insertions and extractions, bringing exceptional firepower and maneuverability to bear.

OPPOSITE:

A-4E Skyhawk over USS *Bonhomme Richard* (CVA-31), Gulf of Tonkin

The nimble Skyhawk served as the Navy's light attack aircraft over North Vietnam, especially in the early part of the conflict. On August 4, 1964, the A-4 of Edward Alvarez was shot down over North Vietnam. Alvarez survived and became the first Navy prisoner-of-war in North Vietnam. Notable A-4 pilots who were shot down and taken prisoner in North Vietnam, included John McCain and James Stockdale.

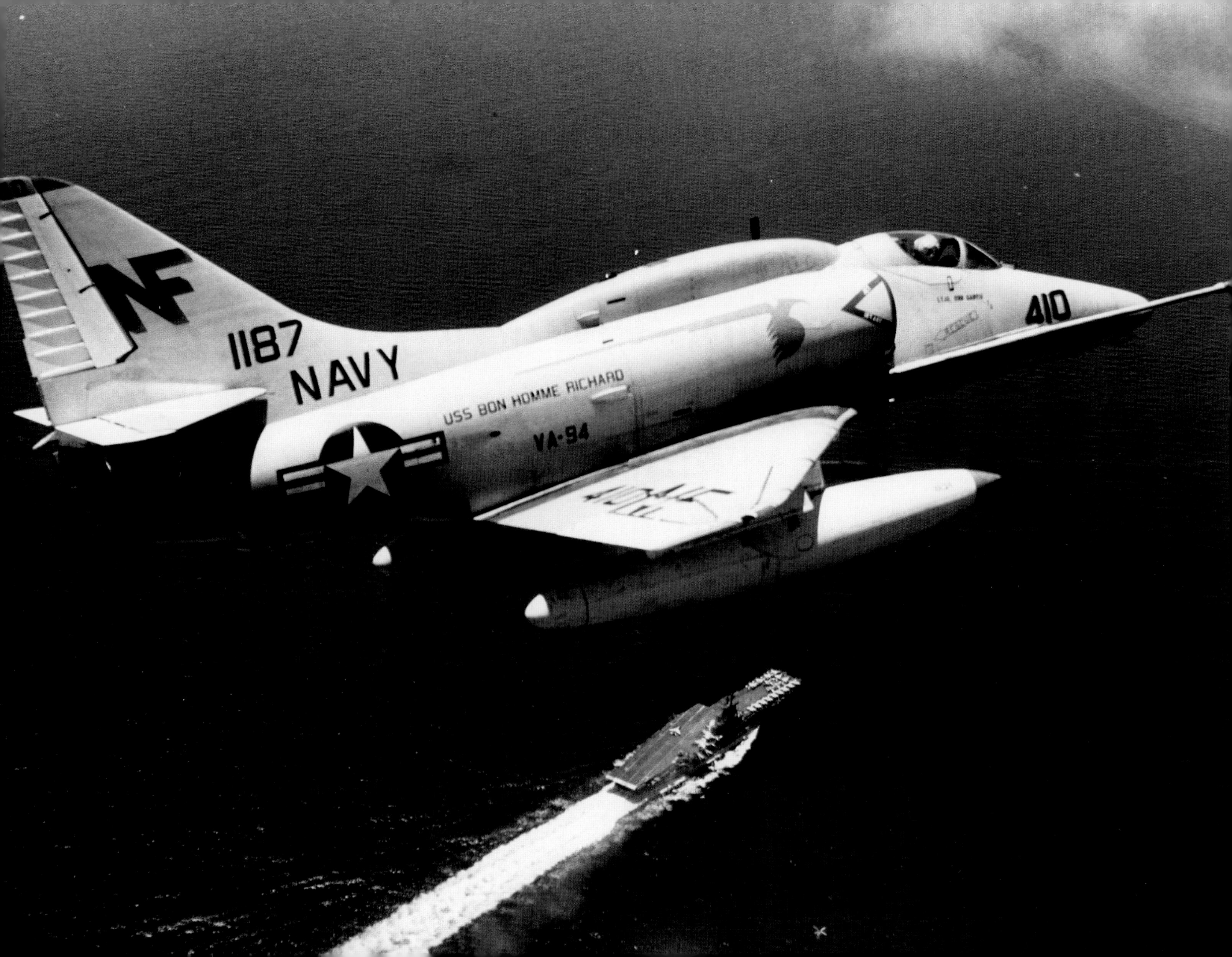

NF
1187
NAVY
USS BON HOMME RICHARD
VA-94
410

USS *Boston* (CAG-1) Fires her 8-inch Guns
Beginning with Operation Sea Dragon in 1966, Navy vessels
sought to disrupt the seaborne Viet Cong supply line. The
famed Ho Chi Minh Trail had a seaborne counterpart that
shipped tons of food and ammunition to the Viet Cong in the
south. In 1966 alone, Navy forces boarded 181,482 watercraft
and engaged in 482 firefights—greatly disrupting communist
supply efforts.

**USS *Garrett County* (LST-786) Operating
in the Mekong Delta**
As efforts to interdict Viet Cong shipping in the brown waters
of the Mekong accelerated, four LSTs were recommissioned
to support and serve as mobile home bases for the river patrol
operations of River Division 10. The versatile ships could tend
both helicopters and Patrol Boats River (PBRs).

LEFT:

Navy F-4B Phantom II drops Mk 82 Bombs

Capable of carrying 18,000lbs (8,160kg) of weapons, the Phantom became a versatile ground-attack mainstay as the Vietnam War raged on. When engaged in difficult ground combat, U.S. troops would call for airpower support and the Phantom was always on hand to tip the balance of battle.

ABOVE:

Phantoms Combine for Operations above North Vietnam

During the Vietnam War the Navy lost 530 aircraft in combat, resulting in the deaths of 377 aviators, with 64 reported missing, and 179 taken as prisoners-of-war.

ABOVE:

Armored Troop (ATC) Carriers on the Mekong River

Trailed in formation by other ATCs and Monitor gunboats, these ships were a formation of the Mobile Riverine Force (MRF). The MRF was a joint Navy–Army endeavor designed to ship troops into battle against the Viet Cong via converted World War II-era landing craft, and supported by the firepower of the gunboats.

The marriage of Navy and Army units was ideal for harassing the nimble Viet Cong, with both troop landings and the application of naval firepower in the watery landscape of the Mekong Delta.

OPPOSITE:

Patrol Craft Fast (PCF) Ships, Mekong Delta

PCFs, also known as Swift Boats, were specifically designed for the uncertain military world of counterinsurgency. All-aluminum construction and shallow draft made the Swift Boat ideal for operating in the narrow and congested waterways of the Mekong. Swift Boats normally operated in groups of three to five, and were heavily involved in both shipping interdiction and the insertion of ground troops, especially SEALs.

RIGHT:

Patrol Boats River (PBRs), Mekong Delta

Smaller and more lightly armed than the Swift Boats, the PBRs formed the backbone of naval efforts to interdict Viet Cong supplies in the Mekong. A typical month of interdiction efforts involved 65,000 hours of patrols by PBRs, 1,500 hours of flight by the "Seawolves," and 80 enemy watercraft destroyed.

OPPOSITE:

USS *Wisconsin* (BB-64) Fires a Broadside

The role of the Navy was critical to the run up to Operation Desert Shield/Storm in the Persian Gulf War of 1990–91. Only the labor of 240 ships carrying 18.3 million pounds of weaponry and supplies made the war possible. As ground operations neared, the naval flotilla, Battle Force Zulu, cleared Iraqi ships from the seas and pounded the coastline, diverting Iraqi attention and supplies from the main landward line of advance.

ABOVE:

Two F/A-18C Hornet Aircraft form up over the USS *Saratoga* (CV 60)

Navy airpower of all types was integral to the success of Operation Desert Shield/Storm. Advanced FLIR thermal sights and 500lb (227kg) laser-guided bombs were a deadly Navy combination. And Navy EA-6B Prowler electronic countermeasure aircraft jammed Iraqi defense capabilities, even while HARM missiles destroyed enemy communications.

RIGHT:

USS *Philippine Sea* (CG-58) Launches a Tomahawk Cruise Missile

Clashes between Albanians and Serbs in Kosovo led to a humanitarian crisis and to NATO intervention in 1999. In the confused situation on the ground, the accuracy provided by the Navy's Tomahawk cruise missiles proved key in the successful conclusion of Operation Allied Force.

OPPOSITE:

F/A-18 Hornets Take off from the USS *Theodore Roosevelt* (CVN-71)

A civil war had broken out in Bosnia after its secession from Yugoslavia between ethnic Bosnians and ethnic Serbs. The resulting massacres of Bosnian civilians resulted in NATO intervention in Operation Deliberate Force in 1995. The first wave of air assaults was launched from the USS *Theodore Roosevelt* (CVN-71), which targeted Serb forces involved in the ongoing humanitarian crisis.

Training

The Navy has a tradition of training sailors for the technical skills required for, and rigor expected of, a life and warfare at sea since the birth of the Republic. The goal of training is first to instill the Navy's core values of honor, courage, and commitment, along with the skills of working in a pressure-packed team environment.

For many, the journey to Navy service begins at Recruit Training Command, Great Lakes, outside Chicago—the Navy's only boot camp. This initial training lasts eight weeks, and involves a battery of everything from classroom academic instruction, marksmanship, water survival, to firefighting. After the eight weeks, successful recruits are able to don the Navy ball cap, indicating acceptance into the world's finest naval force. A second level of training takes enlisted men on the first steps towards their individual careers and occupational specialties. After completion of this training, sailors receive their ratings badges, denoting their individual specialties, which can range widely from aerographer's mate, or hospital corpsman to diver. Training specialty is also denoted by badges worn on the left breast that indicate command, warfare, and other qualifications.

A host of demanding specialty training is also available, ranging from officer training at the United States Naval Academy, to perhaps the most grueling of all military training regimens in Basic Underwater Demolition/ SEAL training in Coronado, California. Especially given today's high tempo environment of worldwide deployment and the deeply technical nature of many of the Navy's specialties, training continues at all levels of command throughout a sailor's career.

OPPOSITE:
Plebes Navigate an Obstacle Course During Sea Trials at the U.S. Naval Academy
Carrying a Combat Rubber Raiding Craft, plebes—as Navy freshmen are known—struggle through an obstacle course as part of the Sea Trials capstone training evolution for Naval Academy trainees. In a brutal test to see if they have what it takes to be a Navy officer, the plebes are physically and mentally challenged, with long-distance group runs, damage control scenarios, water training, and a host of obstacle courses.

LEFT:

Crawling on a High Rope

The obstacles on Navy courses are specially designed to test physical endurance, mental toughness, and split-second decision-making skills. Trainees at all levels dread the obstacle course, but its unique blend of physical and mental challenges help prepare sailors for the rigors and leadership and combat.

RIGHT:

Seabees Cross a Wire Bridge, Jungle Warfare Training Center, Camp Gonsalves, Okinawa, Japan

Tasked with supporting combat operations, humanitarian missions, and disaster relief across the globe, Seabees have to be ready for anything. The endurance course tasks trainees with an assortment of 31 obstacles on a 3.8 mile (6km) course amid the rugged terrain of the Okinawan forest.

LEFT:

Sailors and Marines Compete, Commanding General's Fitness Cup Challenge, Parris Island

Utilizing both competitive spirit and teamwork, the Commanding General's Fitness Cup Challenge pits the services against each other for bragging rights in a host of physical events, from an obstacle course, an endurance run, a combat fitness test, and Humvee pull.

TOP RIGHT:

A U.S. Naval Academy Midshipman Navigates the Low Crawl Obstacle

Of the many obstacles that Sea Trials throws at the plebes, the low crawl portion of the obstacle course is often the most grueling. After running for much of the rest of the course, the plebes have to hit the dirt and slither under wire obstacles, a situation made even worse by adding mud and water to the mix.

BOTTOM RIGHT:

Special Warfare Combatant-craft Crewman (SWCC) Candidates Low Crawl, Naval Special Warfare Center (NSW), Coronado

The NSW is an elite training center and works with sailors who make up the Navy's SEAL and Special Boat Teams. Training is highlighted by "The Tour," a 72-hour endurance event that tests candidate's physical and mental toughness.

ABOVE:

Rope Climb, Sea Trials, U.S. Naval Academy

Since their first admission to the Naval Academy in 1976, female plebes have suffered through the grueling Sea Trials along with their male counterparts. That year, 81 female midshipmen entered the Naval Academy, with Elizabeth Anne Rowe making history as the first to graduate in 1980. Four years later Kristine Holderied became the first female midshipman to graduate at the top of her class.

RIGHT:

Gunner's Mate 2nd Class Zohair Haddad Climbs a Cargo Net, Jungle Warfare Training Center

As Navy training enters the 21st century, the Navy has become more diverse than ever, more accurately reflecting the diversity of the U.S. population. The Navy is now 61 percent white, 18 percent African-American, 9 percent Hispanic, and 12 percent other races. Women make up just under 20 percent of the active Navy and its reserve.

LEFT:

Plebes Lift Telephone Poles
Much of the Navy's training regimen stresses acting as a team under pressure. The log PT station of Sea Trials has the team lift the massive log and then undertake a series of exercises with it.

OPPOSITE:

Basic Crewman Training
Navy training is conducted through a series of iterations from basic through more advanced courses. BCT is the first phase of special warfare combatant-craft crewman (SWCC) training designed to ready sailors for special operations.

OPPOSITE TOP RIGHT:

Basic Underwater Demolition/SEAL (BUDS) Students Log Exercise
During their final week of training, SEALs face "Hell week," a solid week of training with only four hours of sleep allowed per day. When they are at their most exhausted, the SEALs face "Old Misery," a log weighing 400lbs (180kg). Teams have to hoist the log and perform a series of drills.

OPPOSITE BOTTOM RIGHT:

Carrying a Log, Croix du Sud, New Caledonia
Hosted by the French, Croix Du Sud ("southern cross") is designed as a multi-national training for disaster relief that takes place on alternate years.

Chief Petty Officer Selectees Participate in Group Physical Fitness, Perdido Key, Florida
Moving up through the ranks in the Navy always means another battery of training—the higher the rank, the more detailed the training. To become a Chief Petty Officer requires attending the Chief Petty Officer Indoctrination course. The course is now being replaced by continuous education dubbed Enlisted Leader Development Continuum.

Using a Hydraulic Grinder Underwater

Navy training often involves a host of water exercises ranging from basic water survival to water combat. The most specific training regimens of all involve preparing divers to undertake underwater repairs to naval vessels. In dire situations ships cannot make port for repair and must be repaired at sea, no matter what the conditions.

Sailors Participate in Conditioning Training, Joint Base Pearl Harbor-Hickam

Swimming laps has long been considered one of the most effective forms of conditioning. Swimming skills are key to surviving the loss of a ship at sea, and thus are key elements in naval training regimens.

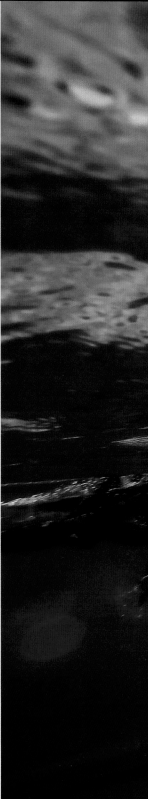

LEFT:

SEALs Train with a Seal Delivery Vehicle (SDV)
Often launched from and retrieved by submarines, the SDV is a submersible designed for the covert insertion of SEAL teams into hostile territory. Underwater training helps the SEALs to thoroughly prepare for these dangerous and complex missions.

OPPOSITE:

SEAL Trainees Participate in Night Gear Exchange
During their second phase of training, SEALs enter the water to exchange all of their dive gear with masks that have been blackened. Such training allows SEALs to undertake complete gear shifts underwater during operations in total blackness.

Joint Operations, Pattaya, Thailand
U.S. Navy and Royal Thai Navy divers prepare to enter the water. The dive was part of a joint dive exercise with the U.S. Navy in Cooperation Afloat Readiness and Training (CARAT). The multinational training scenario takes place every year and primes U.S. naval forces to work effectively with regional allies against naval challenges in the Pacific and Indian oceans.

Members of the Naval Aircrew Candidate School (NACCS) Stay Afloat During a Drown-Proofing Exercise
Naval aviators and air crew receive three weeks of extensive training at the Naval Aviation Survival Training Program facility to aid in their survival in the event of an aircraft being lost at sea.

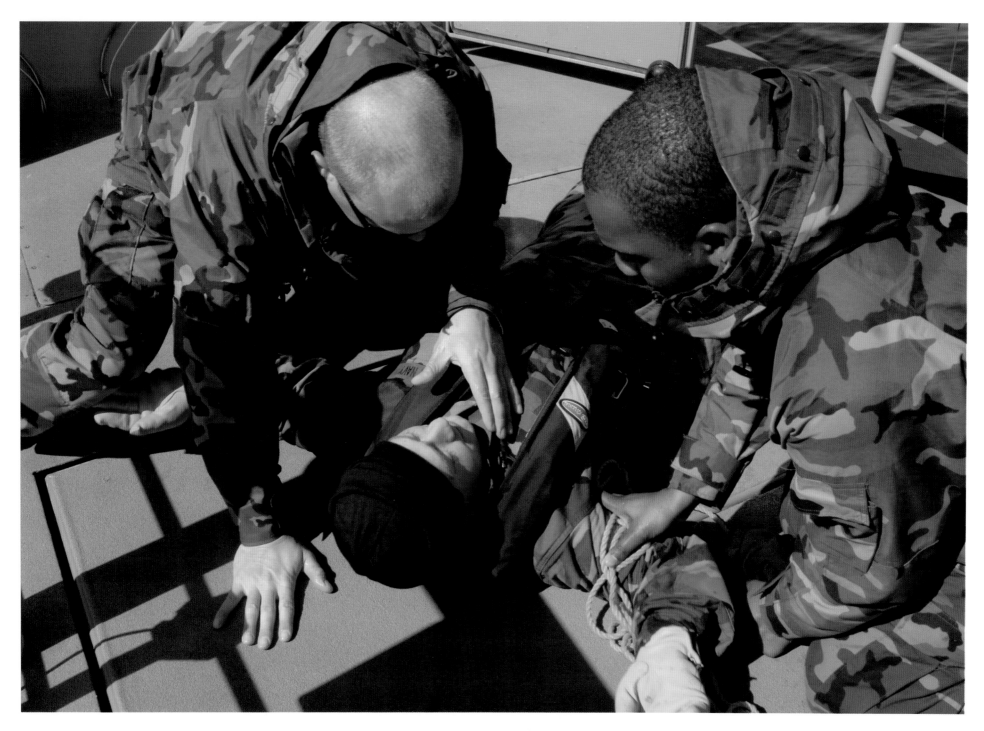

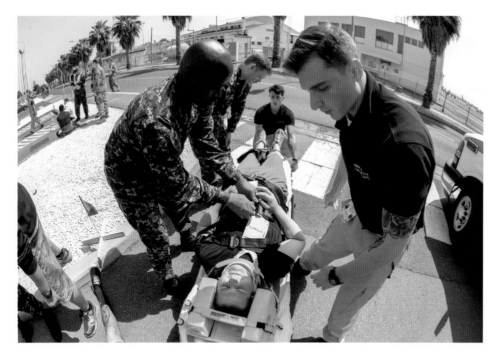

OPPOSITE:
**First Aid Training,
Man Overboard Drill**
The training is part of the
boat team's "Crewman Boot
Camp," a training geared
toward getting the newly
formed boat team qualified on
basic seamanship, weapons,
first aid, and small boat
operations before deployment.

ABOVE:
**Simulated Casualty
Training, Naval Air
Station Sigonella, Sicily**
Training needs to simulate
almost any scenario, in
this case that of an active
shooter on base. These Navy
personnel are prepared to
react to challenges in Europe,
Africa, and Southwest Asia.

TOP RIGHT:
**Naval Air Crewmen
Conduct Shipboard Aviation
Rescue Training**
The unparalleled maneuvering
of a helicopter make it the
perfect platform for rescues at
sea, especially during a fast-
moving naval engagement.
Naval air crewmen train
continuously at their craft
to be fully prepared when
called to action in one of the
most complex maneuvers of
warfare—an air/water rescue
during combat.

BOTTOM RIGHT:
**Culinary Specialist 3rd Class
Yohannis Swaby Attends to
a Simulated Broken Leg**
All sailors receive a basic
training in battle first aid,
rendering them capable of
stabilizing common wounds
in mass casualty situations
or in a situation in which
medical personnel have been
incapacitated. Care of the
wounded aboard ship is
everyone's duty.

LEFT:

**A Navy Instructor Sprays
a Sailor with Pepper Spray**
Facing deployments to trouble
spots across the globe, sailors
receive training in security
operations, crowd control,
and the use of nonlethal
weapons such as pepper spray.
In preparation for using such
weapons sailors first have to
experience their effects.

RIGHT:

**Preparing to Escape the
Multi-Place Underwater
Egress Trainer**
The Aviation Survival
Training Center utilizes the
"Helo Dunker" to simulate a
submerged aircraft fuselage.
Students have to escape from
the rapidly submerging Helo
Dunker in a vital practice of
emergency aircraft escape
at sea.

**Sailor Participates in
a Nonlethal Weapons
Training Course**

Having already been hit with a
dose of pepper spray the sailor
has to fight blind against a
well-padded instructor. As
the situation in the world gets
more chaotic, facing riots or
insurgents becomes an ever
greater possibility for sailors,
necessitating detailed training.

LEFT:

**Midshipmen Conduct
a Ruck March,
U.S. Naval Academy**

The ruck march is one of
the most grueling moments
of a sailor's training during
Sea Trials. Carrying a 50lb
(22.5kg) load (in a ruck),
the trainees must navigate
a rugged march of 12 miles
(19km) in three hours or less.

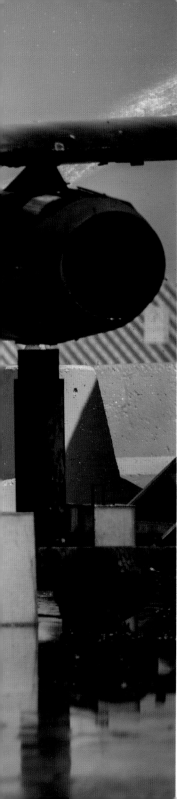

Firefighters at Naval Station Rota (NAVSTA), Spain
During Operation Lazy Altitude, an integrated aircraft-mishap exercise, a mixed international crew—including Navy personnel and the *Bombaderos*, local Spanish firefighters—trains in an integrated force structure. NAVSTA Rota is the largest American military base in Spain, housing Navy and Marine Corps personnel.

Special Warfare Combatant-Craft Crewmen Train Aboard a Rigid-Hull Inflatable Boat
Crewman Qualification Training is a 14-week course that teaches special warfare combatant-craft crewmen candidates the skills they need as members of the Naval Special Warfare boat teams. Candidates learn navigation, craft maintenance and repair, towing, anchoring, and weapons.

Logistics Specialist Fires a .50-caliber Machine Gun During Gunnery Exercise

Live fire exercises are a critical element of Navy training. While never a true predictor of action under fire, such exercises like this aboard the guided-missile destroyer USS *Jason Dunham* (DDG 109), hone onboard gunnery skills.

RIGHT:

Small Caliber Action Team Stands Ready

This crew, aboard the Ticonderoga-class guided-missile cruiser USS *Philippine Sea* (CG 58), trains for a maritime security operations exercise. In the congested waters outside ports on the world's sea lanes, reaction time is key to success.

OPPOSITE:

Mk 38 25mm Machine Gun Live-Fire Weapons Training

The chain-driven auto cannon has the capability of firing up to 500 rounds per minute. It is primarily used for close-in defensive fire against targets such as hostile patrol boats and mines.

ABOVE:

Mineman 1st Class Marion House Fires an M240B Medium Machine Gun

Training ashore at Camp Blanding Joint Training Center in Starke, House serves aboard a littoral combat ship, which is designed to put his training to use in the anti-mine and anti-submarine roles, from deep waters to the coastal littoral.

OPPOSITE:

Builder 2nd Class Steven Arkin (left), Navy Cargo Handling Battalion (NCHB), Fires a 9mm Pistol

In wartime, all sailors must be ready to transfer to a combat role if the situation demands. Being able to handle a variety of weapons and marksmanship is a requirement at all levels of naval readiness.

OPPOSITE:

A Student Naval Aviator Prepares for a Training Flight

Training aboard the T-44C Pegasus aircraft allows for training at all levels alongside a pilot instructor. With two turboprop engines, digital displays, and an integrated flight management system, the Pegaus allows trainee flyers to learn the real world skills required for their future aircraft assignments.

LEFT:

T-44C Pegasus Takes Off at Naval Air Station (NAS) Corpus Christi

If chosen for the Maritime flying route, naval aviators train at NAS Corpus Christi. Training lasts 18 months, with NAS Corpus Christi turning out 400 qualified pilots each year.

Sailors of the Navy Explosive Ordnance Disposal (EOD) Group Descend During Free-Fall Training

Parachute insertion training allows EOD groups rapid and stealthy deployment ability. On the modern battlefield, improvised explosive devices (IEDs) pose a huge threat, and sailors of the EOD group are prepared to evaluate and destroy explosive ordinance, including chemical and nuclear weapons.

U.S. Navy SEALs Train with Special Boat Team 12 on Boarding Gas and Oil Platforms

Oil and gas platforms have proliferated in the world's oceans and have become tactical points of interest in both an economic sense and in the realm of force projection. Quick insertion training, designed to seize platforms before they can be disabled or destroyed, is a critical skill for the SEALs.

Officer Candidate School (OCS) Members Train on the Conning Officer Virtual Environment (COVE) System

COVE allows for a portable training system that can be replicated across the country to allow Conning Officers to train with elements of ship handling in a virtual environment.

Flight Deck Virtual Reality Simulation Trainer

The Carrier-Advanced Reconfigurable Training System (C-ARTS) is part of the Navy's increased focus on virtual reality simulations to augment training for many of the most difficult and dangerous operations aboard ship.

ABOVE:
Small Craft Attack Team Training Aboard USS *Germantown* (LSD-42)
Amphibious dock landing ships, like the *Germantown*, are designed to launch smaller craft into combat. Designed initially to launch hovercraft and helicopters, the vessels have been augmented to launch everything from landing craft to tanks. Training for such a variety of high-pressure operations is designed to be as intense as possible.

ABOVE RIGHT:
A Dog Handler Runs his K-9 Partner Through an Obstacle Course
Training of K-9 teams at the Joint Base Pearl Harbor-Hickam Military Working Dogs Section prepares man's best friend to operate within a Navy environment. Noted for their explosive/narcotic detection capabilities, K-9s play an important role at Navy bases and facilities across the world.

RIGHT:
Special Warfare Combatant-Craft Undergoing Navigation Training
Having to be ready at a moment's notice to deploy to ocean, littoral, or riverine environments worldwide, the training for Special Warfare Boat Operators is varied, and includes weapons, cultural awareness, navigation, planning, intelligence, and medicine. Their jobs call for a combat flexibility that is only achieved through an intense regimen of training.

ABOVE:

**U.S. Navy SEALs Drop into the Ocean
from an HH-60H Seahawk helicopter**

Like their Special Warfare Boat Operator counterparts, SEALs
are an elite force that needs to have a training edge to take on
tasks of all types, from Operation Neptune Spear—the raid
that killed Osama Bin Laden—to the rescue of Captain Richard
Phillips of the *Maersk Alabama* from Somali pirates.

RIGHT:

**A Navy SEAL Climbs a Ladder During a Ship Assault
Training Scenario**

An average SEAL spends more than a year training, including
a 24-week school known as Basic Underwater Demolition/Seal
(BUD/S) training, a parachutist course, and a tactical medical
course. Even after graduation, SEALs undergo a continuous
cycle of training to further hone their already elite skills.

OPPOSITE TOP LEFT AND BELOW LEFT:

U.S. Navy SEALs Exit a C-130 Hercules Aircraft

Every SEAL must pass a highly-regimented, three-week parachute course that progresses from basic static line jumps through accelerated free falls from high altitude carrying heavy equipment. The course completes with a night jump fully loaded with combat gear from a minimum altitude of 9,500ft (2900m).

OPPOSITE RIGHT:

SEAL Students Participate in Surf Passage

Facing the titanic waves off San Diego is part of a SEAL's initial phase of orientation training. Followed by seven weeks of increasingly difficult physical training, seven weeks of combat diving training, and seven weeks of land warfare training, BUD/S training then gives way to parachute training and a further 26 weeks of training in everything from close quarters combat, to demolitions, to arctic skills training in Alaska.

ABOVE:

Recruits March in Formation, Graduation Ceremony

Facing an unprecedented array of challenges across the globe in an uncertain strategic situation, Navy training readies sailors to face everything from technology-driven warfare, to counterinsurgency, to riverine operations, to humanitarian support missions.

Weapons

The Navy is tasked with a bewildering array of responsibilities, ranging from serving as the nation's leading nuclear deterrent; to fielding mobile and forward-based airpower meant to tip the strategic balance in warfare; to winning fleet-on-fleet battles; to landing ground forces on hostile shores; to policing international waterways to halt piracy and terrorism. The huge range of duties means the Navy can deploy an arsenal of weapons that is the most powerful and varied in the world.

At the strategic end of the spectrum sits the Trident II Missile, carried aboard the Navy's ballistic missile submarines, with enough power to destroy entire cities and armies. The Navy's nine carrier strike groups, each deploying up to 90 aircraft, can launch devastating aerial attacks against almost any target on the planet.

The Navy's surface warships carry an array of weaponry from Tomahawk cruise missiles that can hit targets a thousand miles distant, to Phalanx Vulcan cannons that can destroy small ships and incoming anti-ship missiles. The Navy also boasts an entire class of ships designed to carry Marines into littoral combat and that can launch a variety of smaller vessels, from Amphibious Assault Vehicles to Air Cushioned Landing Craft. The Navy also has dedicated mine countermeasures ships. At the lowest end of the tactical spectrum, the Navy fields a range of coastal patrol ships, gunboats, and rigid-hull inflatable boats that perform patrol and interdiction duties, anti-terrorism operations, and troop insertions of SEAL teams. The wide array of ships and weapons, from nuclear submarines to the firearms carried by special operators, make the Navy one of the most versatile weapons of warfare that the world has ever seen.

OPPOSITE:
**Los Angeles-class Attack Submarine USS *Hampton*
(SSN-767) Surfaced at the North Pole**
The submarine was taking part in Ice Exercise, a joint operation with the British Royal Navy operating beneath the polar ice cap. The exercise demonstrates the Navy's ability to freely navigate all international waters. *Hampton*'s motto is *Qui Desiderant Pacem Preparate Bellum*—"Those who desire peace prepare for war."

OPPOSITE:

Nimitz-class Supercarrier USS *Carl Vinson* (CVN-70), Pacific Ocean

Carl Vinson and the Navy's other carriers form the centerpieces of each carrier strike group. The Navy presently fields nine carrier strike groups, each with a single carrier, a cruiser, a destroyer squadron, and up to 90 aircraft. Together the ships of the carrier strike group pack as big of a punch as the entire military force of many nations in the world.

RIGHT:

F/A-18 Hornet, USS *Abraham Lincoln* (CVN-72)

An F/A-18 attached to the "Warhawks" of Strike Fighter Squadron (VFA) 97 conducts a "touch and go" landing and takeoff. Introduced in the late 1970s, and having undergone continual upgrades, the F/A-18 remains a versatile fighter and attack aircraft and an indispensable part of the Navy's ability to project power worldwide. The aircraft's maneuverability and durability make it ideal for everything from fleet air defense duties, to air interdiction, to air support for ground operations.

MH-60S Seahawk Helicopter Approaches the Flight Deck of the USS *Dwight D. Eisenhower* (CVN-69)

Based on the same design as the Army's UH-60 Black Hawk, the Seahawk has folding main rotor blades and a hinged tail to reduce the space it takes up aboard ship. One of the Navy's workhorses, the Seahawk is deployed on ships ranging from frigates to supercarriers. While the Seahawk pictured is taking part in a vertical replenishment drill, the Seahawk is a multiuse aircraft capable of undertaking anti-submarine roles, troop insertions, medical evacuations, and search-and-rescue missions.

OPPOSITE:
Aviation Ordnancemen Download a CATM-9 from an F/A-18C Hornet
The use of training weapons like the CATM-9 allow for critical practice in assembly, loading, and unloading. On board the aircraft they are used to train in target acquisition and tracking.

RIGHT:
An SH-60F Seahawk Approaches the USS *John C. Stennis* **(CVN-74)**
In its anti-submarine role this Seahawk is armed with both a multimode radar and an airborne low frequency sonar. Once contact is made, the Seahawk can utilize one of its MK 54 lightweight torpedoes or its .50 caliber guns. In an anti-ship mode it is armed instead with Hellfire anti-surface missiles.

LEFT:

MH-60R Seahawk Lifts off the Flight Deck of the USS *Ronald Reagan* (CVN-76)
The Seahawk carries advanced electronic support measures to detect threats, a forward-looking infrared system for low light targeting, and a chaff and decoy dispenser for baffling incoming missiles. It also has dual redundant, ballistic hardened flight controls to allow for increased survivability.

OPPOSITE:

EA-18G Growler, USS *Harry S. Truman* (CVN-75)
Replacing the workhorse EA-6B Prowler, the Growler now serves as the Navy's primary electronic warfare aircraft. It carries three dedicated radar-jamming pods and a communications countermeasures system, including a high radiated power-jamming transmitter. The Growler carries air-to-air missiles and HARM high-speed anti-radiation missiles. Its maximum speed is Mach 1.6 (1230 miles per hour).

ABOVE:

AV-8B Harrier Launches from USS *Tarawa* (LHA-1)
The only short takeoff vertical landing jet in the U.S. military, 22,000 pounds of thrust enables the Harrier to hover like a helicopter and then leap forward at nearly supersonic speeds. The Harrier's supreme maneuverability makes it one of the most versatile aircraft in the Navy's arsenal.

OPPOSITE:

Communications Personnel Record Flight Operations Aboard USS *Nimitz* (CVN-68)
In addition to the flight deck personnel, including the "yellow shirts," who choreograph the comings and goings of aircraft on deck, within the ship are a host of electronic systems that are akin to those used by civilian air traffic controllers to track aircraft launches and landings, to control the often crowded airspace on and above the carrier.

Enterprise Carrier Strike Group (CSG), Atlantic Ocean
One of the mightiest weapons of war ever seen, the _Enterprise_
CSG includes the aircraft carrier USS _Enterprise_ (CVN-65),
guided-missile frigate USS _Nicholas_ (FFG-47), guided-missile
cruiser USS _Leyte Gulf_ (CG-55), destroyer USS _McFaul_
(DDG-74), Military Sealift Command fast combat support
ship USNS _Supply_ (T-AOE-6), and the guided-missile
destroyer USS _James E. Williams_ (DDG-95).

ABOVE:

Catapult Officer Signals the Launch Order for an F/A-18F Super Hornet

Usually ending his hand signals with a flourish, the "Shooter" has the final say over aircraft launches from carriers. Capable of carrying up to 90 aircraft, modern supercarriers bring the Navy's power to most corners of the globe.

RIGHT ABOVE:

Arresting Gear Crew Replace a Cross Deck Pendant

Aircraft retrieval is one of the most dangerous moments of carrier service. Naval aviators approach the carrier at 130 knots, with the carrier itself often moving at a speed of 20 knots while pitching and rolling in the seas. Add in the "burble" of wind turbulence created by the carrier's own superstructure, and the critical nature of the arresting gear becomes clear.

RIGHT BELOW:

Aviation Ordnancemen Upload a GBU-38 Bomb to an F/A-18C Hornet

The GBU-38 is a 500lb (226kg) Joint Direct Attack Munition (JDAM) that uses a standard Mk-82 bomb and was developed for precision bombing in urban warfare. An integrated inertial guidance system, coupled to a Global Positioning System receiver gives the GBU-38 a range of 15 nautical miles and precision accuracy in all weather.

OPPOSITE:

USS *Montgomery* (LCS-8) Launches a RIM-116 Missile

The RIM-116 rolling airframe missile (RAM) is a lightweight, infrared, surface-to-air missile that is mainly used as a point defense weapon against incoming anti-ship missiles. It reaches speeds in excess of Mach 2.5 (1900mph) and is over 95 percent accurate.

RIGHT:

Aviation Ordnanceman Fires a .50-caliber Machine Gun, USS *Tripoli* (LHA-7)

In the modern world of asymmetric warfare, the most dire naval threats are often posed by mines, fast patrol boats, attack swimmers, and even pirates. Against such close-in threats automatic weapons are the defensive measure of choice.

OPPOSITE:

An AV-8B Harrier Hovers above the USS *Bataan* (LHD-5)
In Operation Iraqi Freedom (OIF) the *Bataan* served as "Harrier
Carrier." During the main portion of OIF, Harriers logged 3,000
flight hours in a total of more than 2,000 individual sorties.

ABOVE:

**USS *Bonhomme Richard* (LHD-6) Launches
a RIM-7 Sea Sparrow Missile**
Introduced into service in 1976, the Sea Sparrow has undergone
several improvements. A ship-to-air missile, the Sea Sparrow is
designed for close-in defense against both enemy aircraft and
sea-skimming missiles. It remains an important part of a layered
naval defensive system.

OVERLEAF:

**MV-22 Osprey Lands on Amphibious Assault Ship
USS *Wasp* (LHD-1)**
Long in use by the Marine Corps and valued for its versatility
because of its vertical takeoff and landing capabilities, the
Osprey is being added to the Navy arsenal. Its superior range
and lift capability make the Osprey a prime platform for vertical
replenishment roles.

ABOVE:
Helicopters Aboard the USS *Iwo Jima* (LHD-7)
Iwo Jima demonstrated its versatility in 2005 by sailing up the Mississippi River in the devastating wake of Hurricane Katrina. There it became the command center for relief operations and served as the area's only functional base for helicopter operations, making over 1,000 flights in the process.

RIGHT:
Amphibious Assault Ship USS *Kearsarge* (LHD-3)
The Wasp-class amphibious assault ships are some of the most versatile in the Navy's arsenal. With a range of over 9,000 miles (14,500km), *Kearsarge* can carry up to 12 landing craft, which can land a compliment of over 1,500 troops. It also launches an assortment of fixed-wing and rotary-wing aircraft, carrying up to 20 Harrier aircraft.

A Sailor Rests Aboard the Supercarrier USS *Theodore Roosevelt* (CVN-71)
Named for the 26th President, who was a leading proponent of naval power, the ship was the first of its kind to be built using modular construction, which sped the process by 16 months. Launched in 1988, *Theodore Roosevelt* has been a mainstay of the Navy, with its first major deployment taking place in Operation Desert Shield, in which its aircraft took part in 4,200 sorties, dropping 4,800,000lbs (2,177,243kg) of bombs.

**F/A-18E Super Hornet
Flies over the Kajaki Dam
Reservoir, Afghanistan**
The aircraft was a part of
the compliment aboard the
USS *Dwight D. Eisenhower*
(CVN-69) supporting
Operation Enduring Freedom.
Launched in 1975, *Eisenhower*
has undergone several
upgrades, and in 2013 led the
first U.S. strike group that
included an allied ship, the
German frigate *Hamburg*.

ABOVE AND RIGHT:
Navy Littoral Combat Ship USS *Independence* (LCS-2)
Featuring an innovative trimaran hull and lightweight aluminum
construction, *Independence* can reach speeds of nearly 50 knots
and has a range of 10,000 nautical miles. Unlike traditional
ships with fixed armament, *Independence* instead carries
tailored mission modules that can be configured to different
mission goals, making the ship supremely versatile.

Amphibious Assault Vehicle (AAV)
Launching from the well deck of the Amphibious Dock Landing Ship USS *Comstock* (LSD-45), the AAV is a fully tracked amphibious landing vehicle and serves as the main troop transport for the U.S. Marine Corps. The *Comstock* can carry and launch up to 36 AAVs, each capable of carrying a compliment of 21 Marines into battle.

RIGHT:
Rolling Airframe Missile Launcher
With its compliment of Marines, the USS *Gunston* (LSD-44) has to be able to defend itself against attack and carries an armament of two 25mm Mk 38 cannons, two 20mm Phalanx Vulcan cannons, a Rolling Airframe Missile launcher, and six .50 caliber machine guns.

TOP LEFT:

Guided-missile Cruiser USS *Antietam* (CG-54)

Like the sister ships of it's Ticonderoga class, the *Antietam* is a multiuse warship. It's Mk 41 Vertical Launch System, aided by the information provided by the Aegis Combat System, can launch Tomahawk missiles to strike strategic targets, anti-aircraft missiles for fleet defense, or anti-ship missiles.

BOTTOM LEFT:

USS *Princeton* (CG-59) Fires Mk 45 5-inch Gun

Manned by a crew of six (gun captain, panel operator, and four ammunition loaders), the Mark 45 can fire 20 rounds a minute with a maximum range of 13 nautical miles.

ABOVE:

F/A-18s Fly over the Guided-Missile Cruiser USS *Mobile Bay* (CG-53)

The *Mobile Bay* is assigned to the *John C. Stennis* Carrier Strike Group (Strike Group 3). During Operation Enduring Freedom, *Stennis* led a multi-country international fleet that included ships from Italy, France, the United Kingdom, and the Netherlands.

OPPOSITE:

MH-60S Sea Hawk Helicopters Deliver Cargo to USS *Harry S. Truman* (CVN-75)

In distant operations, replenishment at sea via helicopter is a critical task for sustainment. During such operations, ships are at their most vulnerable, making the role of support ships— here, the USS *Gettysburg* providing the helicopters— of paramount importance.

OPPOSITE LEFT:

USS *Benfold* (DDG-65) Fires a Surface-to-Air Missile

One of the early Navy ships to be fitted with the Aegis Ballistic Missile Defense System, *Benfold* was the first ship to successfully and simultaneously engage an incoming ballistic missile and a cruise missile.

OPPOSITE RIGHT:

USS *John S. McCain* (DDG-56) Fires a Surface-to-Air Missile

Guided-missile destroyer *John S. McCain* fires a surface-to-air missile during a training exercise. The versatile Sparrow missile has all-weather, all-altitude operational capability and can attack high-performance aircraft and missiles from any direction. During the exercise, the missile intercepted a remote controlled, GPS-guided test drone.

RIGHT:

Launching USS *Paul Ignatius* (DDG-117)

One of the Navy's newest Arleigh Burke class guided-missile destroyers launched in 2019, *Paul Ignatius* features an Aegis 9 Baseline combat system that allows the ship to simultaneously patrol for ballistic missiles as well as combat traditional air and cruise missile threats.

MH-60S Sea Hawk Delivers Cargo
As part of the Naval Fleet Auxillary Force, *Alan Shepard* and its sister ships are tasked with delivering ammunition, provisions, and mechanical supplies to naval ships afloat—in this case, the USS *Rafael Peralta* (DDG-115). USS *Alan Shepard* has a speed of 20 knots, a range of 14,000 nautical miles, and can carry 5,910 long tons of cargo.

USS *Zumwalt* (DDG-1000)
The *Zumwalt* utilizes stealth technology that makes its radar signature look more like a small fishing boat. The unique shape of the ship and the use of composite materials reduces radar return. Modified propeller shapes and muffled exhaust systems reduce noise produced by the ship; it also boasts limited electronic emissions, and reduced heat exhaust emissions.

BELOW:

Guided-Missile Destroyer USS *Arleigh Burke* (DDG-51)

Among *Arleigh Burke*'s many combat features is the Collective Protection System (CPS). Through the use of decontamination stations, advanced filters, airlocks, and programmable logic controllers, the CPS is able to filter out chemical, biological, and radioactive particles so the ship can operate in contaminated battle environments.

OPPOSITE:

Cyclone-class Coastal Patrol Ships Conduct Fleet Maneuvers

Designed for coastal patrol and interdiction surveillance, Coastal Patrol Ships also provide mission support for SEAL operations. The ships are armed with 25mm Mk 38 autocannons, the MK 19 automatic grenade launcher, a series of machine guns, and stinger missiles.

RIGHT:

Amphibious Transport Dock Ship USS *New York* (LPD-21)
Designed to embark and land troops in expeditionary warfare missions, 7.5 tons of steel was salvaged from the rubble of the World Trade Center in the construction of the *New York*'s bow.

OPPOSITE:

Navy Gunboat, Persian Gulf
A navy gunboat patrols the Persian Gulf near Camp Patriot while USS *Nassau* (LHA-4) is anchored in the background. In congested waters, nimble craft are required to screen against attacks by the small vessels of opposing forces like the Iranian navy.

OPPOSITE:

Rigid-Hull Inflatable Boat and the Coastal Patrol Ship USS *Typhoon* (PC-5)
Based out of Bahrain, *Typhoon* is part of the Navy's Fifth Fleet, which is responsible for actions in the Persian Gulf, the Red Sea, the Arabian Sea, and part of the Indian Ocean. The volatile and traffic-heavy nature of these areas make the roles of small craft like *Typhoon* especially important in its interdiction role. Telling friend from potential foe in crowded waters is key to both avoiding incidents and protecting U.S. interests.

RIGHT:

Live-Fire Exercise, USS *Monsoon* (PC-4)
A sailor practices with a .50 caliber heavy machine gun. Training by firing at simulated hostile small boats during an Advanced Phase Training Exercise (APTEX) stresses the ability to first discern friendly vessels from hostile and then accuracy in defensive fire.

LEFT:

AN/SQQ-32 Sonar
A sailor operates the AN/SQQ-32 variable depth mine hunting detection and classification sonar. The sonar operates from a towed body tethered to the ship that can be controlled from the Sonar Maintenance Room. It includes two active sonars that can detect and classify mines on the surface, in the water column, or at the bottom of the sea.

OPPOSITE:

Mine Countermeasures Ship USS *Pioneer* (MCM-9)
MCS utilize remotely-operated mine disposal systems and vehicles to locate and destroy mines. The vehicle uses high resolution sonar and low light level television to locate mines, and then cable cutters and explosive charges to destroy them.

OPPOSITE TOP LEFT:

SEALs Operate Desert Patrol Vehicles (DPV)

Built by Chenowth Racing Products, the DPV is powered by a 200 horsepower engine and can reach 60mph (90km/h) while carrying 1,500lbs (680kg) of supplies. Each "Dune Buggy" is outfitted with complex communication and weapon systems designed for harsh desert terrain.

OPPOSITE LOWER LEFT:

A SEAL Armed with a SCAR

In 2004 U.S. Special Operations Command put out a call for a new family of Combat Assault Rifle (SCAR). SEALS use a newer variant of this powerful and versatile weapon, that has barrel options for close-range combat, long-range engagements, and as a grenade launcher.

OPPOSITE RIGHT:

SEALs in a Combat Rubber Raiding Craft (CRRC)

The CRRC can be launched from shore, afloat, from aircraft, and from submarines. When stored, it takes up little space and then can be inflated by a foot pump, compressor, or CO2 tank. Its superb buoyancy and resilience makes it capable of operating in everything from rough seas to small tributaries.

BELOW:

SEALs Conduct Clandestine Insertion Training

Naval Special Warfare (NSW) has more than 1,000 special operators and support personnel deployed to more than 35 countries. Continuous training and forward basing make the SEALs ideal for rapid reaction to worldwide threats. These SEALs are armed with the Close Quarter Battle Receiver (CQBR), a compact assault rifle used by the Navy and valued for its effectiveness in confined spaces.

LEFT:

Ohio-class Ballistic-missile Submarine USS *Alabama* (SSBN-731)

The Ohio class are the largest submarines in the Navy, each carrying 24 Trident II missiles, each of which can be loaded with up to eight Mk 5 re-entry vehicles each with a 455 kiloton warhead. The Navy's 14 ballistic-missile submarines carry roughly half of America's active thermonuclear warheads.

RIGHT ABOVE:

Sonar Control Room, USS *Normandy* (CG-60)

A Ticonderoga-class guided-missile cruiser, *Normandy* is designed for surface-to-surface, surface-to-air, and anti-submarine warfare. During the Persian Gulf War in 1991, *Normandy* demonstrated its versatility by firing 26 Tomahawk missiles at Iraqi ground targets.

RIGHT BELOW:

USS *Winston S. Churchill* (DDG-81) Undergoes Replenishment at Sea

Launched in 1999, *Churchill* acknowledges America's chief ally and is named in honor of the famed World War II leader of Great Britain; it is the first modern Navy ship to be named in honor of a British citizen. It is fitted with the 62-caliber Mark 45 naval gun system, has a reduced radar signature, and is armed with Tomahawk, surface-to-air, and anti-submarine missiles.

OPPOSITE:

USS *Missouri* (SSN-780) Departs Pearl Harbor
The Virginia class of attack submarines are the Navy's newest, expected to be procured and built through 2043. The Virginia class replaced the nascent Seawolf class in part by costing $1 billion less per unit—though it takes over nine million labor hours to produce each Virginia class submarine.

ABOVE:

Trident II Missile, USS *Maine* (SSBN-741)
An unarmed Trident II (D5LE) missile launches from Ohio-class ballistic missile submarine USS *Maine* from beneath the surface of the Pacific, 2020. The Trident missile system is carried by 14 Ohio-class submarines, each armed with thermonuclear warhards that can wreak huge destruction.

RIGHT:

USS *Newport News* (SSN-750)
The Los Angeles-class *Newport News* departs the harbor at Souda Bay, Crete, following a port visit. In 2007 the *Newport News* was involved in a collision with a Japanese tanker in the Arabian Sea, when the venturi effect caused the submarine to rise in the water as the tanker passed overhead.

TOP LEFT:

USS *Jimmy Carter* (SSN-23)
The third and final submarine of the Seawolf class, which was designed to replace the Los Angeles class. Designed to counter the threat posed by Soviet ballistic submarines, each Seawolf carries up to 50 Tomahawk missiles and has eight torpedo tubes for launching the Mk 48 guided torpedo. Once the Cold War ended, though, the U.S. opted for the smaller, but still powerful, Virginia class.

BOTTOM LEFT:

USS *Florida* (SSGN-728)
In 2003 *Florida* was converted from a ballistic missile submarine, with more of a strategic role, to a cruise missile submarine, with more of a tactical role. With the conversion the submarines could carry 155 Tomahawk cruise missiles. *Florida* demonstrated its might in Operation Odyssey Dawn in 2011 by launching 93 Tomahawk missiles against Libya, to begin the enforcement of a no-fly zone.

RIGHT:

USS *Alexandria* (SSN-757)
Alexandria submerges under two feet of ice near the North Pole. The Los Angeles class of nuclear submarines have proven their worth in the Navy for decades, with some achieving an active service life of over 40 years.

Operations in the 21st Century

The Navy has been involved in active operations for nearly the entire 21st century. After the terrorist attacks of 9/11, it fell to the Navy to quickly bring retaliatory power to bear in Afghanistan by deploying salvos of Tomahawk cruise missiles. Carrier groups were then tasked with continuous air support to Operation Enduring Freedom—a deployment that continues today. As attention shifted to Iraq, the Navy gathered the might of five carrier groups to strike Saddam Hussein's military with waves of air assaults and Tomahawk cruise missile strikes in a "shock and awe" campaign that quickly neutralized the effective resistance of the Iraqi armed forces.

As the wars in Afghanistan and Iraq dragged on, the Navy transformed its operational role first to one of ground support to U.S. troops in the field and then to a counterinsurgency role that put heavy emphasis on riverine operations and the use of specialized SEAL teams. Finally, as the U.S. began to disengage from Operation Iraqi Freedom and Operation Enduring Freedom, the Navy's role transformed again to one that emphasized training of local Afghani and Iraqi forces to enable them to transform battlefield victory to strategic gain. Twenty years of deployment have tested the Navy, but as always the Navy has persevered and stands ready for the next call to action.

OPPOSITE:
Joint Operations in the East China Sea, 2018
Amphibious transport dock ship USS *Green Bay* (LPD-20) (foreground), amphibious assault ship USS *Wasp* (LHD-1) (center), and the Japan Maritime Self Defense Force Osumi-class amphibious transport ship JS *Shimokita* (LST-4002) (background) conduct bilateral maneuvers as part of the United States' longstanding commitment to its allies in East Asia.

LEFT:

USS *Philippine Sea* (CG-58) Launches a Tomahawk Cruise Missile

Demonstrating the long reach of the Navy, *Philippine Sea* launched the first U.S. counterstrike against the Taliban in Afghanistan with this nocturnal Tomahawk launch on October 7, 2001.

ABOVE:

F-14 Tomcat, USS *Carl Vinson*, Operation Enduring Freedom

The carrier was rounding the southern tip of India when its orders were changed in the wake of 9/11. On October 7, 2001, *Carl Vinson*'s aircraft launched the first air strikes on Al-Qaeda targets. In the coming 72 days, *Carl Vinson* and Carrier Wing 11 launched 4,000 sorties over Afghanistan.

OPPOSITE:

F/A-18 Super Hornets over Afghanistan, 2008

These aircraft are members of Strike Fighter Squadron 31, known as the "Tomcatters." The second-oldest Strike Fighter Squadron in the Navy, established in 1935, the Tomcatters flew 3,100 sorties and dropped 59,000lb (26,760kg) of ordinance in close air support of Operation Enduring Freedom in 2008.

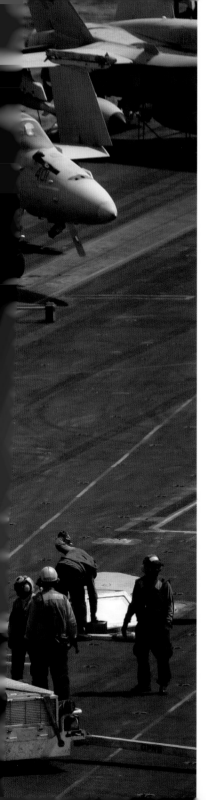

LEFT:

F/A-18 Hornets, USS *Eisenhower* (CVN-69)
Navy crewmen gather around a line of F/A-18 fighters on the
deck of the USS *Eisenhower* in the Arabian Sea, 2010. In 2016,
Eisenhower was at the forefront of U.S. operations against
ISIS (Islamic State of Iraq and Syria). During *Eisenhower*'s
deployment its aircraft dropped 1,100 bombs on ISIS targets,
crippling the terrorist group's infrastructure.

ABOVE:

**Ordnancemen Load an AIM-7 Sparrow Missile
on to an F/A-18 Hornet**
The Sparrow has been the air-to-air missile of choice for the
Navy since the Vietnam War. It has been upgraded with an
inverse monopulse seeker for more precise active radar homing.
In the Persian Gulf War (1990–91) there were 40 Sparrows fired,
with 30 hitting their targets with a high kill rate.

OPPOSITE:

Carrier Strike Group in the Persian Gulf

USS *Nimitz* (CVN-68) and the guided-missile cruiser USS *Philippine Sea* (CG-58) steam in formation during a Strait of Hormuz transit, September 2020. The Nimitz Carrier Strike Group is deployed to the Fifth Fleet area of operations in support of naval operations to ensure maritime stability and security in the Central Region, connecting the Mediterranean and the Pacific through the western Indian Ocean.

TOP RIGHT AND BELOW RIGHT:

Landing Craft Air Cushioned (LCAC)

Pictured top right, an LCAC rushes past USS *Nassau* (LHA-4) in the Persian Gulf. Marines of the I Marine Expeditionary Force were critical to the quick victory against Iraq's military in March and April 2003. Bottom right, an LCAC arrives at Camp Patriot, Kuwait, to load Marines and supplies.

FAR RIGHT:

"Shock and Awe"

A Tomahawk cruise missile streaks toward Iraq from the USS *San Jacinto* (CVL-30). On the night of March 21, 2003, 30 Navy ships and submarines launched 320 Tomahawks in a night of "shock and awe" that overwhelmed the Iraqi defensive network. The Navy carried a total of 1,000 Tomahawks to the invasion of Iraq in 2003.

TOP LEFT:

Afterburners on Deck

An F/A-18 hits the afterburners as it is launched from the USS *Constellation* (CV-64) in the Persian Gulf. As the Navy readied for Operation Iraqi Freedom, it gathered the might of five carrier groups to play its considerable role in the invasion, including the *Theodore Roosevelt* and the *Harry S. Truman* in the eastern Mediterranean and the *Constellation*, *Kitty Hawk*, and *Abraham Lincoln* in the Arabian Gulf.

ABOVE:

Airplane Launching System

Sailors are engulfed by steam generated by the airplane launching system on the deck of the Nimitz-class aircraft carrier USS *Carl Vinson*, Western Pacific, 2018.

BOTTOM LEFT:

Bomb Load

Navy weapons ordnancemen wheel bombs to aircraft on the deck of the USS *Constellation*. Before the invasion of Iraq, *Constellation* had been active in patrolling the no-fly zones over Iraq, leaving its pilots extremely familiar with the area and its many potential targets.

OPPOSITE:

Sand Storm

Flight deck personnel aboard the carrier USS *Kitty Hawk* (CV-63) prepare aircraft for an incoming sand storm. Weather in the Persian Gulf area is notoriously fickle, and on March 25, 2003, a low-pressure cyclonic storm drew in massive amounts of dust and sand from as far away as Egypt. The storm persisted for three days, grounding aircraft, with sand fouling engines and causing havoc for operations.

**Washing Down USS
Abraham Lincoln (CVN-72)**
With the prevalence of
blowing dust and sandstorms
in the Middle East, ship
maintenance, while still
mundane, takes on a life and
death significance. The fine
sand and dust particles can
have a great impact on the
delicate flight systems of
aircraft, especially helicopters.
Dust storms are blamed
for three out of every four
chopper accidents in Iraq
and Afghanistan.

LEFT:
**Airfield Security,
Air Force One**
A SEAL team helps secure the airfield as Air Force One lands at Al Asad Air Base, Iraq, in 2007. President George W. Bush was arriving to meet with Iraqi and U.S. officials, including General David Petreaus, in the wake of the successful surge against insurgent forces in Iraq.

TOP RIGHT:
A Navy SEAL Watches a Munitions Cache Being Destroyed in Afghanistan
The SEALs discovered the munitions while conducting a Sensitive Site Exploitation (SSE) mission in Eastern Afghanistan in 2002. On the modern asymmetric battlefield, munitions caches are key to insurgency and its use of mines and improvised explosive devices (IEDs). Locating and destroying such caches are a prime mission for the SEALs.

BOTTOM RIGHT:
SEAL Advisors, Afghanistan
Armed with a SCAR assault rifle, a Navy SEAL takes up a defensive position in a village in northern Zabul province, Afghanistan. As Operation Enduring Freedom continued in 2010, the mission changed more and more to advising Afghan National Army soldiers, including these SEALs operating against drug lords in Afghanistan.

**Night-time Missile Strike
on Libya, 2011**

Seen through night-vision
lenses aboard amphibious
transport dock USS *Ponce*
(LPD-15), the guided-
missile destroyer USS *Barry*
(DGD-52) fires Tomahawk
cruise missiles in support of
Operation Odyssey Dawn in
March 2011. This was one
of approximately 110 cruise
missiles fired from Navy ships
and submarines that targeted
approximately 20 radar and
anti-aircraft sites along Libya's
Mediterranean coast. Joint
Task Force Odyssey Dawn was
the U.S. Africa Command task
force established to provide
tactical control of forces
supporting the international
response to unrest in Libya.

**USS *Gabrielle Giffords*
in the South China Sea**

The USS Independence-
variant littoral combat
ship USS *Gabrielle Giffords*
(LCS-10) conducts routine
operations in the South
China Sea, June 2020. Part
of Destroyer Squadron 7,
Gabrielle Giffords was on
a rotational deployment,
operating in the Seventh Fleet
area of operations. Based in
Yokosuka, Japan, the Seventh
Fleet is the largest of the
forward-deployed U.S. fleets,
with 60–70 ships, 300 aircraft
and 40,000 Navy and Marine
Corps personnel.

ALL PHOTOGRAPHS ON THIS PAGE:

Boarding Teams

Pictured top left is a team from the amphibious assault ship USS *Boxer* (LHD-4). On April 8, 2009, Somali pirates attempted to seize the *Maersk Alabama*. After the failed attempt, the pirates took Captain Richard Phillips and fled in a lifeboat. Foiled by SEALs, a team from *Boxer* towed the lifeboat in to be processed for evidence.

Pictured left, a visit, board, search, and seizure team from the USS *Halsey* (DDG-97) approaches a Yemeni *dhow* in the Indian Ocean. Such teams go through eight weeks of specialized training. The teams operate in waters crowded with small vessels

and combat terrorism, piracy, and smuggling.

Pictured above, a boarding team from the USS *Chosin* (CG-65) point to a suspected pirate *dhow*. In areas where states have failed, including the Horn of Africa, piracy abounds. Policing the sea lanes is both a strategic and tactical necessity for the Navy.

OPPOSITE:

River Patrol

Navy riverine craft poised for action on the Shatt al Arab River, Basra, Iraq. Control of the river, which is formed by the confluence of the Tigris and Euphrates rivers, was key to shutting down the terrorist supply network in Operation Iraqi Freedom.

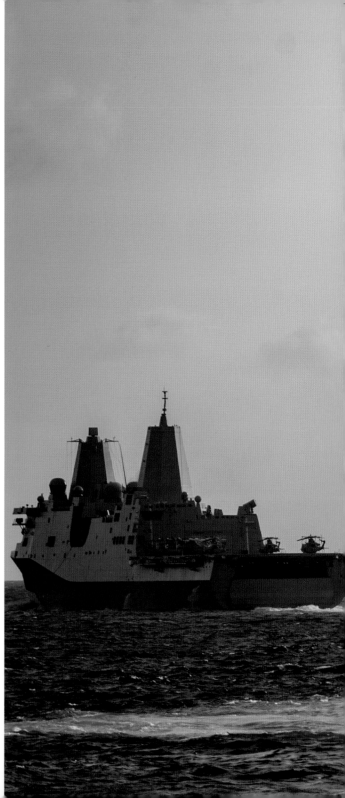

ABOVE:

Air Traffic Controller, USS *Abraham Lincoln* (CV-72)
A Navy Air Traffic Controller monitors the local airspace
in the Traffic Control Center of the USS *Abraham Lincoln*
(CV-72). In all conflict situations, control of the active
airspace is at a premium.

RIGHT:

***Theodore Roosevelt* Carrier Strike Group
in the South China Sea, 2020**
Ships from the *Theodore Roosevelt* Carrier Strike Group and
the *America* Expeditionary Strike Group transit the South
China Sea, March 2020. Operating as an expeditionary strike
force, the Navy-Marine Corps team integrates the combat
power of the USS *Theodore Roosevelt* with the flexible
capability of the *America* Expeditionary Strike Group and 31st
Marine Expeditionary Unit, to provide the fleet commander
with a capable, credible combat force that can be deployed
anywhere in the world.

LEFT:
Atlantic Deployment
An MH-60S Sea Hawk
assigned to Helicopter Sea
Combat Squadron (HSC) 5
and an MH-60R Sea Hawk,
assigned to Helicopter
Maritime Strike Squadron
(HSM) 74, prepares to take
off from the flight deck of the
USS *Gerald R. Ford* (CVN-78)
somewhere in the Atlantic
Ocean, 2017.

ABOVE:
**Birds-eye View of the USS
Gerald R. Ford (CVN-78)**
F/A-18F Pilot Jamie R. Struck
approaches the Navy's newest
carrier, USS *Gerald R. Ford*
(CVN-78), off the Virginia
coast. Delivered in 2017 and
beginning deployment in 2020,
Gerald R. Ford is the first of a
new class of carriers designed
to upgrade the Navy's
capabilities and replace the

ageing Nimitz-class carriers.
Four more carriers are under
construction. Currently the
world's largest carrier with a
displacement of 100,000 tons,
Gerald R. Ford will include
many improvements over the
Nimitz class, such as replacing
traditional steam catapults
with the Electromagnetic
Aircraft Launch System
(EMALS) for launching
combat aircraft.

Picture Credits